# KEEPING CALM

**Also by Faith Winters**

Abundance
Abundance Workbook

Connections
Connections Workbook

Fundamentals
Fundamentals Workbook

Keeping Calm
Keeping Calm Workbook

Restoration
Restoration Workbook

# KEEPING CALM

*Seven Key Skills to Being Calm in the Midst of Troubling Times*

**Faith Winters, LPC**
**Timothy Winters**

www.FaithfulHabits.com

**KEEPING CALM**

Seven Key Skills to Being Calm
in the Midst of Troubling Times

Author: Faith Winters
Contributing: Timothy Winters



Editor: Rochelle Dean

First Printing: December 2020

Faithful Habits Press
www.faithfulhabits.com

Paperback ISBN: 978-1-7367367-0-8

Library of Congress Control Number: 2021903805

Minor portions of this book were originally published within other books by Faith Winters.

Contact the author at: faith@faithfulhabits.com

For information about discounts for bulk copies for groups contact: info@faithfulhabits.com

# Why Read this Book

**Would you like to face life's troubles with confidence?**

**These seven skills can transform your life!**

When you read this book you will discover how to unlock the secrets of how naturally calm people:

- Have a calmer, happier life
- Make better decisions
- Get rid of constant anxiety
- Lower the effects of stress
- Get better rest and sleep

If you apply all the skill in this book you can be a calm person more powerfully in control of yourself and able to move through life with confidence, no matter what is going on around you.

**Are you ready to make lasting change?**

**Get the new KEEPING CALM workbook to help strengthen your specific calm goals.**

This companion workbook shows you step by step how to develop and strengthen the key skills for living a calmer life using easy-to-follow exercises that you can complete at your own pace.

## Written by a leading expert with more than 20 years' experience

**Faith Winters** is a Licensed Professional Counselor in Oregon, USA, a Mental Health Professional. As an Approved Clinical Supervisor, Faith has trained many other mental health professionals. She is an expert who has taught thousands of people how to live calmer, more fulfilling lives. She is an author of books focused on helping people to heal and grow.

**Additional material by Timothy Winters,** Faith's son, who has a bachelors degree in Technology Management. He has helped lots of people understand and use their technology in ways to make their lives better. Timothy has provided tech support for over 15 years.

# Contents

*A calm*

*and modest life*

*brings more happiness*

*than the*

*pursuit of success*

*combined with*

*constant restlessness.*

*Albert Einstein*

# CHAPTER ONE

## What This Book is About

**Life is uncertain.** Are you tired of worrying and feeling anxious? Do the uncertainties of life weigh you down? These are troubling times: extreme weather events, social unrest, pandemic, health concerns, job stress, unemployment, recession, relationship struggles, and parenting concerns abound. Many of us are trying to deal with today's issues while also worrying about tomorrow's troubles. Sometimes it is just one problem, but other times problems bombard you, stacking one on top of another until it feels like they are weighing you down. All these problems can add to your stress until your calmness simply fades away.

Yet there are some people who never seem to be ruffled. No matter what is going on in their lives, they always keep their calm. Have you ever wondered where they get the strength to do it? You *want* to feel alive, calm, and happy despite the chaos,. You want your life to have meaning and purpose. You would like to have time to relax without a feeling of dread in the back of your mind.

This book is about how to keep calm in the midst of troubling times. Read on to learn seven key skills of how to have a calm life, no matter what is happening in it.

The solution to feeling uneasy is not solving all the problems you feel anxious about. The solution is learning how to build within yourself the resilience to face life's trouble with an unshakable calm. Calmness is a learned skill anyone can acquire. Just like many triggers can cause stress and anxiety, many different skills help to lower stress and improve calmness. Some are physical skills, some are mental skills, some are about habits, inputs, attitudes, values, some are about planning and the choices you make. Any of these can affect your mental well-being and your sense of being calm.

By picking up this book, you have already taken a step on the journey to a calmer life. You recognized the concern and took action to address it. The next step is to learn and apply these principles.

At the beginning of learning new skills, it can take ten units of effort to get one unit of benefit in return. As you keep going, it gets easier. Eventually, you can even get ten units of return for putting in one unit of effort! During my journey towards a calmer life, I found that to be true. As I implemented the first calming skills, calmness in my life spread even to areas I had not yet approached. As I got stronger, I found that my anxieties became less troubling.

In some ways, it is like a child learning to walk. When my son was just beginning to pull himself up by the front of the sofa, I would put a toy a few inches out of reach. He would reach for it, struggling to move toward it, and often gravity would pull him down. He would bump his nose and cry. I would comfort him and encourage him to try again, putting the toy just a little out of reach. He would try again and fall again. Why would I keep putting that toy just out of reach, so he had to struggle? I knew that while he was struggling to walk toward the toy, he was learning how to balance and how to handle gravity and his legs were growing stronger. I knew that soon he would not only able to walk, but to run. He was soon running, dancing, and playing with gravity.

When we bounce balls, slide, and swing, we are playing with gravity. That same force that used to bring us down is still there, but our ability to handle gravity has changed. It no longer seems to fight our every move. Now we move easily through it and even have fun with it. We can do the same thing with the problems that arise in our lives, not only surviving them, but enjoying our life, too.

I have three main qualifications to help you in your journey to a calmer life:

- Experience in living for decades with struggles – growing up in traumatic circumstances and dealing with anxiety, panic attacks, and PTSD (Post Traumatic Stress Disorder) for decades. I discovered my first calming skills while coping in the midst of those painful years. Later, I went through a healing process in therapy where I learned more calming skills as the anxiety ended, the panic attacks ceased, and the PTSD was finally gone.

- Education—I then attended university to get a master's degree in counseling so I would have the professional therapeutic skills to help others heal from trauma. Through those years of specialized education and the 3 more years of supervised training I became a licensed professional counselor.
- Experience in teaching these key skills to others—I have taught thousands of people how to live better lives and how to keep calm in the midst of struggles.

In my time as a therapist, I have worked with hundreds of individuals, hearing their stories of a life hindered by anxiety and worry. I have helped them develop the skills presented in this book and I have seen lives transformed. People who were crippled by deep levels of anxiety made dramatic changes and moved toward a calmer life. I have also developed and taught workshops to thousands of people.

Not only am I a professional therapist, trained in how to help people make behavioral change. I also have lived a life filled with anxiety, worry, panic, and

PTSD. Yet as I made changes, I experienced healing and grew into a calm life with abundant happiness. As a person who has suffered much, I want there to be less suffering and pain in the world, and more calm and happiness. I want that for you!

This book contains tried and true methods of how you can make changes to have a calmer and happier life. I will be sharing the principles of what I have discovered, experienced, been taught, studied, and developed. If you address the emotional, physical, and intellectual principles presented in this book, you can live your very best life, unhindered by debilitating levels of anxiety.

If you implement two or three of the principles found in these pages, you will experience a calmer, happier life. It will take some effort on your part, but the skills you need to move forward are here in your hands. If you apply five or six of these ideas, it can literally change the course of your life and have a positive effect on people around you. If you apply all the skills, you will discover a revolution inside, a return to something even more powerful than calm. That is the presence of peace.

These are not ideas for only a favored few. You do not have to be rich or brilliant. All of us can apply these principles: rich or poor, brilliant or ordinary. I promise that when you are done reading this book and have implemented some of these skills, you will feel calmer and more confident in your ability to face life's trouble.

This is not just a collection of ideas that worked for me. It is what worked for my clients, for the participants in my groups and classes. Thousands of people have used these skills to grow toward a better life. You can apply these skills in your own life as well. You will be able to discover not only the hidden sources of stress and worry, but the many ways in which anxiety affects our lives. You will learn the principles of calmness and peace. You will understand that calmness is more than an outward appearance; it is an outflow of a solid inner strength.

*Calm is a superpower.*

***Brené Brown***

*"If you can keep your head*

*when all about you*

*Are losing theirs*

*and blaming it on you, …"*

***Rudyard Kipling***

# CHAPTER TWO

## Overview of a Calm Life Versus an Uneasy Life

What does it mean to be calm? A calm person is not taken over by worry, anger, or excitement. A calm person is more powerfully in control of themself and more able to face life's troubles. Calm people are not under the control of strong emotions like anger, fear, or anxiety even when there is cause for it. A calm person helps others to be calmer just by the calm way they face circumstances.

### Examples of an uneasy life

The only time Jessica feels at ease is when she's sleeping. But even then, her sleep is often troubled by a sense of restlessness. She often wakes up with a feeling of dread. The trouble and worries of yesterday come flooding back in and threaten to overwhelm her. While getting dressed, the anxiety builds. She gets her child ready for school, listening to his constant questions and chatter, trying not to be grumpy with him. It is a welcome relief when he is at school, and she did not have to hold her anxiety down to keep from taking it out on him.

But in the quiet moments, the worries creep back. How will she get the work done? Will the boss be satisfied with the way jobs are completed? Will the money come in on time? Jessica dreads time with co-workers. It means more stress, gossip, unfinished tasks, and requests for her to do things she feels unqualified for or has no time to complete.

She worries about her child; will he be able to make friends at school? Will he get his schoolwork done on time? Did he bring his backpack? Will he be healthy? Is he going to catch a cold or flu from other kids? What if he brings illness home? How will she work if she gets sick?

Going to church Sunday morning should be a time of joy and peace. Instead, Jessica feels more uneasiness: Will she get there on time? Where will she park? Is she dressed appropriately? Will her son behave himself? Will she find friends to talk to? Where will she sit? What does she need to shop for on the way home?

James always feels tired. It is a struggle to wake up. Today, he is certain something bad is going to happen. He goes to get dressed and finds no clean clothes. He feels late, so he rushes out the door, driving through a fast-food restaurant to get something to eat. He is frustrated that a bus pulls in front of him and it seems like it's taking forever to get anywhere. He has to take an unfamiliar route to avoid construction. James is sure he would be late for work again. His boss will be mad. When he gets there, he rushes to start his workday.

He is stressed as he tries to figure out what he needs to do. His coworker comes by and says a comment that he takes as a negative omen. Later, when one thing goes wrong, he thinks, "Oh no. The whole project is going to be ruined. This task will not be done on time." His stress overwhelms him. He's afraid his boss will fire him, and he would find himself living on the street. When James leaves work, he just wants to get home and rest, but his journey is in rush-hour traffic. The vehicles crawl forward, and all he hears is horns honking and angry voices. There are all kinds of hindrances: buses, construction, an accident that slows all traffic to a stop. James is fuming, talking to himself. "Why can't people drive faster? Why does everybody have to be on the road right now? Why does it have to be like this?"

By the time James gets home, he is angry and exhausted. Someone asks him a question and he brushes them aside with a huff. He feels too stressed to deal with anything else. He just wants to sit down and watch some entertainment. However, on the news are images of disasters and trouble. When he finally goes to bed, he struggles to fall asleep. He tosses and turns, knowing tomorrow will be yet another bad day.

**Examples of a calm life**

Charlotte lives a calm life. She has learned key skills to being calm in the midst of trouble. She takes each day as it comes. She gets up, rested from a good night's sleep. Mornings are a peaceful start to the day. She enjoys the morning banter with her family. She gets ready with anticipation of a good day ahead. When thoughts come up about health and finances, she is at ease because she knows how they will be handled. She can focus on her work and takes pleasure in completing each task.

In the quiet moments, Charlotte thinks of all the things for which she is grateful. Work time is busy and often chaotic, but she remembers the big picture of how this work will benefit others and she feels at peace as she completes tasks. She has friendly interactions with co-workers and finds fulfillment in learning new skills to become better at her job. Every day, Charlotte feels pleasure in her work.

Charlotte finds joy in her relationship with her child. They have fun times together. He enjoys his time at school, he completes his classwork, even when it is a struggle. He has friends to share good times with. Charlotte and her son spend time planning and doing home chores together, so they have more time for fun.

Sunday morning is a joyful anticipation of seeing friends, worshiping God, and learning more about relationship with Him and others. The time in study, fellowship, and singing gives her a sense of renewal.

Charlotte's life still has lots of issues: Stretched finances, some health challenges, work stress, social difficulties, and struggles with her son's needs. But her attitude is calm in the midst of the troubles. Anxiety no longer wears her down; she feels peace and joy every day.

Gary wakes up refreshed in the early morning. Getting dressed is easy since clean clothes fill his closet. He knows he will be appropriately dressed for his day since the wardrobe system he uses makes that automatic. After a leisurely breakfast, he leaves for work. Traffic is heavy because there is an accident ahead, so he takes an alternate route he knows. There is road construction, but it is not stressful because he allows plenty of time to travel and still get to work early. When he arrives at work, it's easy to park since he is early. He greets coworkers with a smile as he starts the tasks of the day. He knows what his projects are and has a plan to get them done. He enjoys the creativity of his job. Stresses and issues arise, but he has plans for how to deal with them. When his coworkers are upset, he listens to them without joining them in that heightened emotional state.

On the journey home, traffic is heavy, but he expected it, so he listens to music or an audiobook. He uses this travel time to mentally leave work at work. The music or audiobook helps him to rest even in the midst of traffic. When he parks at home, he takes a couple of minutes to be grateful for his home and family. Those few minutes help him be present with his family, ready for social time, food, and the evening's activities. He and his family share fun and laughter. They go to bed early so they will get enough rest to start a new day. Gary's life has a lot of struggles, but his attitude of calm lowers a lot of the accompanying stress. Troubling times are all around him, but they don't take away his peace. He is able to go through it all with all the energy he needs.

### Calm vs. Uneasy

Feeling uneasy is draining. It saps our energy; it erodes our strength. Think about the amount of effort each person used in those stories. Contrast of the calm day versus the uneasy day. Which of these people put more effort into their day? Which ones felt emotionally depleted and exhausted at the end of each day? It was those who felt uneasy, right? Going through an uneasy day drains energy.

It takes effort to change your life, but living in the same old uneasy life takes effort too. By putting effort into changing, you can change your future toward a life that uses a lot less effort. While learning the key skill of how to be calm does take energy, integrating the principles of calmness into your life is not hard. Living a calm life takes so much less energy than living a life filled with uneasiness.

There are many words to describe the opposite of "calm." To be uneasy, which is to have uncomfortable feelings of anxiety, to worry, to be afraid or stress in ways that hinder your life.

Other words for "not calm" include agitated, ruffled, perturbed, upset, disturbed, turbulent, angry, nervous, irritated, aggravated, panic attack, nervousness, excited, jittery, distracted, disoriented, confused, troubled, unrest, frenzied, depressed, violent, anguished, apprehensive, edgy, impatient, insecure, restless, shaky, tense, scared, unsettled, alarmed, dismayed, harassed, in turmoil, perplexed, perturbed, tormented, and upset.

In this book we use the word uneasy (uneasiness, unease) to refer to all these feelings of "not calm."

Since words have meanings and I want my message to be clear, let us look at a few words and their meanings as they are used in this book. Stress, anxiety, fear, and worry are neither good nor bad. They are neutral descriptions of emotional states. The functional level of any of these are designed to serve a purpose; to warn us of a possible danger so we can prepare or protect; to motivate us to complete a project. While a dysfunctional level hinders rather than helps, being something that is malfunctioning and does not work the way it should. Below, we will discuss each of these feelings and what they look like at functional and dysfunctional levels.

**Anxiety** is a feeling of uneasiness or dread, typically about something with an uncertain outcome.

- **Functional levels of anxiety** can be a source of strength, used as stimulation to be more aware, more diligent, and more alive. Like a person going to a new place becomes more aware of everything around them.

- **Dysfunctional levels of anxiety** can disrupt daily life, creating overwhelming feelings of emotional distress, restlessness, fatigue, difficulty concentrating, irritability, and trouble sleeping.

**Worry** can be defined as giving way to anxiety or unease, or allowing your mind to dwell on difficulty or troubles.

- **Functional levels of worry** can make you more goal-oriented, organized, and self-disciplined. Thinking ahead for possible negative events can motivate you to plan for ways to handle problems and live safer and more effectively.

- **Dysfunctional levels of worry** can make you unhappy and torment you, leaving your mind stuck in a repetitive cycle of thinking about how terrible everything is and how it will only get worse. You have trouble moving forward or having any energy to do anything at all.

**Fear** is a distressing feeling aroused by the anticipation of danger or awareness of threat, evil, pain, etc., whether the threat is real or imagined.

- **Functional levels of fear** are protective. They are what keep us from stepping in front of a speeding bus.
- **Dysfunctional levels of fear** may be crippling. They can keep us from doing anything, even from stepping out of our door.

**Stress** is a feeling of tension that can cause physical, emotional, or psychological strain. Stress can come from any event or thought that makes you feel frustrated, frightened, angry, or nervous.

- **Functional levels of stress** challenge us to grow and change, similar to when we do weight lifting or other types of physical exercise we are stressing our muscles so that they will grow stronger.
- **Dysfunctional levels of stress** can cause damage and be overwhelming. Unremitting stress can erode our health, like the harm that happens when muscles are pushed well past any normal limit.

### Changing Uneasiness

We may ask ourselves if change is even possible. The answer is, "it depends." In life, we have changeables and unchangeables. I cannot change where I was born, when I was born, or the parents I was born to. I cannot change what I experienced as I was growing up. Some things are a mixture of changeable and unchangeable. I cannot change the body structure, height, or bone configuration I was born with. However, I do have some ability to change the amount of weight I put on that frame. There are many things in my life I do have the power to change. I can change my mental, emotional, and physical responses to the stresses of my daily life.

Anxiety and worry are normal responses to the stresses in life, but different people may respond with different intensities to the same stressor. There are functional responses and dysfunctional responses to anxiety and worry. Your uneasy response in any situation is caused by your mind's interpretation of the possible dangers. Much of the way any individual responds depends on past experiences and childhood exposures to stress. We absorb how the important people in our lives responded to stress. Temperament also plays a role in your responses to stress. Finally, we come down to the individual choices you make and whether you choose to handle stress in the same way you've been taught or whether you choose to make a change.

The process of change starts with the desire to change. You have already made a step on the journey by reading this book. You will learn to assess the way the current lack of calm is affecting your life, looking at the sources of those uneasy feelings and behaviors, and then beginning to replace your uneasy responses with calmer ones. As you continue to read through these chapters and implement even a few of these principles, your life will begin to move toward more calmness. Treatments for strongly held feelings of unease may often be helped by using a combination of talk therapy with a mental health professional and sometimes medication. This book can be helpful when used along with therapy in sessions with a mental health professional as you move through these changes.

Building the skills of a calmer life has many different aspects: body, mind, emotions, habits, environment, inputs, attitudes, values, prevention and planning. Learning how to change is different for each aspect we work on. What all the aspects have in common is assessing the current function, deciding what to change, building hope by creating a vision of how you would like this to be after you change, then planning step by step the way forward to move toward your goal.

Change is hard. Let us get that thought out of the way to begin with. Do a little exercise. Put your hands together, fingers interlaced. Do it again faster and once more even faster. Now look at which thumb is on top. Now put your hands together again, with the other thumb on top. Do it again, faster. Was that easy? Did it feel unfamiliar? Did it take intentional effort? That was only a tiny change, too. So, when changing bigger things, expect to put in some effort.

Calmness has many components, including a physical component, a mental component, and an emotional component. These components are interrelated and something that triggers one will have an effect on the others . Think about a time when you were almost in a vehicle accident. What happens in that close call? An adrenaline reaction affects you physically. Your body is suddenly ready to do what you need to do to survive this. It's not an intentional decision; that is just what happens.

We also have the mental component, where we tell ourselves a story about what happened, what the implications are, and the way that we should respond to it. That story we tell ourselves is one that is going to affect what we feel. We have physical feelings—the adrenaline reaction in the body—and then we have the emotional feelings, which come from what we tell ourselves.

When we respond, it triggers feelings in us, and those feelings reinforce our response. We can choose what our response is, and we can choose what the story we tell ourselves about the event is and how we are going to get through it. The story we tell ourselves is going to affect our level of calmness or our level of uneasiness.

Calmness has many components and within each of them is a set of individual skills you can develop that will help to get you through life making better decisions, having less distress, and having better relationships. Moving forward toward a calmer life consists of making a choice. After making the choice, moving forward happens step by step. The journey of 1,000 miles begins with a single step. Your journey toward a calmer life has already begun as you chose to read this book. Before we move into the skills to make lasting changes, let's explore a few ways to get quick relief right now.

*The nearer you come*

*to a calm mind*

*the closer you are*

*to strength*

*Marcus Aurelius*

# CHAPTER THREE

## Get Relief Right Now

**Quick start guide to becoming calmer in 10 minutes or less**

Before we move into the details of the seven key skills of being calm in the midst of troubling times, let's start with a short exercise to improve your calmness level immediately.

Shut off all distractions for the next ten minutes. Do not do this while driving or operating machinery. Quiet or shut off all devices. Close the door. Step away from people to be by yourself.

**Step 1 - Be aware of how you feel.**

On a scale of one to ten, with one being very calm and ten being very uneasy, how would you rate your level of calmness right now? **Step 2 - Manage your body:**

Posture

- Stand or sit up straight, both feet flat on the floor. Straighten your back. Think of being taller, shoulders back, head held high.

Breathing

- Take a deep breath. Let it out slowly.
- Now take in another deep breath through your nose as you slowly count to four.
    - One.... Two.... Three.... Four....
- Pause, holding that breath, for a slow count of four.
    - One.... Two.... Three.... Four....
- Let the breath out slowly through your mouth to a slow count of four.
    - One.... Two.... Three.... Four....

Repeat this exercise four times in a row.

**Step 3 - Manage your mind:**

- Sit with your feet on the floor, sitting up straight, head held high. Breathing comfortably. Close your eyes and think of something pleasant for a few moments: Perhaps a place in nature you enjoy, a color that makes you happy, the soft touch of stroking a loving animal, etc. Spend the full time intentionally focusing on that pleasant thought.

- Take another deep breath and open your eyes.

**Step 4 - Be aware of how you feel.**

On a scale of one to ten, with one being very calm and ten being very uneasy, how would you rate your level of calmness right now?

How much calmer are you than 10 minutes ago?

This exercise is a quick way to lower anxiety and feel calmer immediately. How long that calmness will stay with you varies from person to person, situation to situation. But you can use these techniques as often as you need to begin to be calmer. Learn why this helps and how to make it even more effective by reading the rest of this book.

**Bonus Tip - Physical activity**

Another quick way to feel calmer is by physical activity, moving your body. Taking a brisk walk, while counting to three hundred. Walking outside in nature is best, but walking around the room, or upstairs and downstairs, will work as well.

There are many other techniques you can use to bring more calm into your life: other ways to manage your mind and body, train your thinking, shift your environment, manage your time, face the world, and interact with others. Within this book, I will show you how to gain lasting calm. Now is the time to begin learning the seven key skills to help you live a calmer life even in the midst of troubling times.

## Building Calming Skills

Our physical and emotional feelings of calm or unease are triggered by many things: sights, sounds, smells, and thoughts. It can seem like you do not have control over your own feelings. However, you can influence your feelings by the way you move, the way you think, the situations you put yourself in, the entertainment you watch, the activities that you do, and the company you keep. You can build the skills to change your feelings in many ways, including intention thoughts, physical activity, posture and media or entertainment inputs. We will discuss this in more depth as we go along.

*The ideal*

*of calm*

*exists in*

*a*

*sitting cat*

*Jules Renard*

# CHAPTER FOUR

## Managing Your Body - Skill 1

One part of being calm means managing your body, which involves both the physical and emotional. When you intentionally manage your body you are building a key skill to have more control over your state of calm or unease.

Body uneasiness is a feeling of being physically uncomfortable, not being able to rest, or agitated. Sometimes your chest feels tight, breathing becomes labored, your muscles tense, butterflies flutter in your stomach, pain radiates in your abdomen, your heart pounds. Body uneasiness can cause a feedback loop into uneasiness in your mind where you have a feeling of being uncomfortable, not being able to rest, or like there is a faint gray mist between you and the world, or like hearing an annoying background noise that you cannot quite identify. And because your mind feels uneasy it can add to the uneasiness in your body and cause further emotional distress. And the feedback loop may intensify the feelings.

Fortunately, as you learn how to manage your body toward calmness in this section, it will also help move your mind toward calmness, since the feedback loop works both ways.

Effects of Posture

Posture is important because your body knows the emotions that go with each posture, so even if you are feeling calm when you go into a hunched slump, your body can take on that emotion. If you are in an aggressive, angry posture, your body may take on those emotions.

By simply shifting your posture, you can make a small shift in your emotional state. Take the time to notice when you are feeling calm and confident. Examine what your posture is like in that moment. Later, when you are feeling uneasy, you can remember your calm posture and shift physically to help you to shift emotionally. Being calm is about a lot of layers that work together to help you feel calmer. One of these layers is about physical calm. Not all the layers are required to become calmer, but the more layers you can use, the calmer you will feel.

Stress is a normal part of life. A healthy amount of stress is even good for us: it keeps us focused and alert. When we exercise we are stressing our muscles in a way to strengthen them. However, chronic stress can be debilitating, and intense stress may have negative effects on mind and body. Stress is not just about what is happening; it is also about what we think is happening and the meaning we make of that. Panic attacks are a sudden episode of extreme fear and may trigger both intensely physical and mental reactions with no apparent cause.

Physical fear

Physical fear is the normal reaction of the body to perceived danger. For example, extreme heights may cause a physical adrenaline response in the body, a feeling in the pit of the stomach, muscles tightening, etc. That adrenaline response is getting us ready for fight or flight or freeze or submit. Feeling uneasy can affect performance. Athletes are aware of the effects of physical unease. When the physical fear response is chronically triggered it may lead to negative physical effects or even to making you more susceptible to long term ailments.

Physical Calm

Good posture affects how calm or uneasy we feel. Calm posture is sitting or standing up straight, shoulders back. It is an attitude of confidence, comfortably aware, relaxed, at ease, yet confidently ready for whatever the world is going to bring. This type of posture lets you move forward easily.

Uneasy posture may be hunched down, the slumped back, shoulders raised a bit as if you were expecting a blow. It can be a curled up posture as if trying to protect, hide, or disappear. Another kind of uneasy posture is an aggressive stance, arms crossed, a glaring look, daring anyone to cross you. Uneasy posture can be agitated, nervous, or constantly in motion. When you are feeling defeated or depressed, notice your posture. See what your posture looks like when you are feeling angry and aggressive. All of these physical postures can add to a feeling of mental and emotional uneasiness.

### Deep Breathing

Another component of being calmer physically is breathing deeply. The amount of oxygen we are taking in can affect our feelings of calm or unease. If we have our shoulders hunched, and we are slumped it can restrict the amount of space our lungs have to breathe and so it is harder to breathe deeply. When you stand up straight, sit up straight then it is easier to take in a deep breath.

In the quick start guide we introduced you to 4 by 4 breathing. That is a simple, but an effective skill you can use anytime, anywhere to be physically calmer. Take in a deep breath through your nose to a slow count of four, try to hold that breath for a slow count of four, breathe out through your mouth to a slow count of four, and do that four times in a row.

The effect of 4 by 4 breathing is more than just changing your physical state. It helps you to shift your posture to a calm pose. When you breathe in deeply, you are giving your lungs more air, so there is more oxygen in your blood. When more oxygen gets to your brain, you can think clearer and feel better. Additionally, the counting takes your attention away from uneasy thoughts swirling in your head: the things you need to do next, the things you have not done yet, the things that might happen. These thoughts are set aside for a moment while you count and pay attention to your breathing. Thus, counting and paying attention to your breathing distracts you from what you were thinking about and helps you shift into a calmer mental state. The result is you are physically calmer, mentally calmer and emotionally calmer.

**Skill 1 Managing Your Body**

To summarize, skill 1 is managing your body, which involves both your physical body and emotional state since these feed on each other. When you intentionally manage your body, you are also influencing the state of your mind and emotions. Building the skill of managing your body will give you more control over your state of calm or unease.

- Physical Calm - Practice good posture, walking, standing, or sitting.
- Emotional Body Calm - Breathe deeply.

*To bear trials*

*with a calm mind*

*robs misfortune*

*of its strength*

*and burden.*

*Seneca*

# CHAPTER FIVE

## Managing Your Mind - Skill 2

The second essential skill of being calm is about managing your mind, which involves mental images, selective focus, curiosity and laughter. When you intentionally manage your mind, you are building a key skill to have more control over your state of calm or unease.

Uneasiness in your mind is a feeling of being uncomfortable, not being able to rest, or like there is a faint gray mist between you and the things you need to know, or like a feeling of dread that you cannot quite identify. It may be caused by stress, worry or it may be hard to identify exactly why you are uneasy, but the feeling is there. Mental uneasiness can cause you to begin to take on an uneasy physical posture, affecting how your body feels. As we discussed in the section on Managing Your Body, there is a feedback loop here. When your body feels uneasy it can add to the uneasiness in your mind and cause further emotional distress.

As we mentioned in the first section, we are fortunate the feedback loop works both ways. So, as you learn how to manage your mind toward calmness in this section, it will also help move your body toward calmness as well.

## Mental Images

Just as deep breathing can have a profound effect on your body, mental images can have a profound effect on your mind. Our brain uses many kinds of images, such as emotional images, word images, and picture images. We visualize what something will be like, telling ourselves a story about what has happened, what is happening and what will happen.

When we think, "This is going to be bad; this is going to really be a struggle; it is going to be a disaster," we establish images in all our senses—emotions, sounds sights, etc.—with that thought. When we give that thought of home, make it welcome, and spend time with it, the images we associate with it affect our mental and emotional state, which alters the calmness or unease that we feel.

When we spend time with thoughts of unease, we begin to feel uneasy. Because we feel uneasy, we think more uneasy thoughts, and it can become a vicious circle of ever-increasing uneasiness. When we do the opposite, intentionally thinking about images of calmness and pleasure, thinking this is pleasant, this is nice, this will be good, we establish positive images in all our senses. When we give positive images a home, make them welcome and spend time with them we become calmer.

Try it right now. First, rate your level of calm or unease on a scale of 1 (very calm) to 10 (very uneasy). Then pick one of the following descriptions of a calm place and immerse yourself for a few moments in the sights, sounds, smells, taste, and touch of that calm place. Really relax into the images. Then rate your level of calm again after you complete the exercise. What differences did you notice?

Go to **www.faithfulhabits.com/keepingcalm** for FREE Resources

These descriptions of calm places, and others, are read aloud for you by the author, so you can close your eyes and just imagine the places.

**Ocean**

The horizon spreads in a panoramic in front of you, nothing but water as far as the eye can see, till water and sky merge into a distant blur. Waves come rolling in, swells building till the wave crests and splashes over. An occasional wave grows bigger than the ones before it. They splash down and lap at your feet on the sand. The sky is a saturated blue, dotted here and there with fluffy clouds. Birds bob on the ocean. Little sandpiper birds dash in and out of the surf, playing at the water's edge. Seagulls fly across the blue sky. Listen for their calls. Hear the splashing of the water around your feet. Take a deep breath, smell the salt in the air, taste the freshness of the breeze that blows through your hair, caressing your skin. Feel the water lapping at your feet and splashing. Feel the wet sand as the water rushes over you, pulling the sand out from under your feet. Turn and walk away from the water. Feel the damp sand above the waterline, how firm it is to walk on. Move on until loose, dry sand shifts with each of your steps. Notice how soft the sand and water feel and yet look at the rocks that have been polished smooth by those same elements. The entire feeling at the ocean is one of beauty and soothing peace.

**Forest**

The path between the trees is narrow and dappled with sunlight and shadow. Birds flit back and forth between the trees. Their songs and the swoosh of their wings fill the air. Insects and butterflies flutter and land on leaves swaying in the breeze. Large trees are surrounded by smaller saplings and bushes. The bark of the big trees have deeply grained texture while the bark on saplings is almost smooth. Reach out and touch it. Feel the tree against your skin. Then look up, where the undersides of the leaves sparkle as sunlight shimmers through them. Glimpse the dappled blue sky beyond the canopy. The wind blows and the leaves of different trees dance and flutter in their own unique dances. Beneath your feet lie the fallen leaves of verdant forest, rustling softly as you walk along. Here and there in the treetops, a squirrel skitters along, watching and chattering. The air smells of growing things, rich and earthy. The whole forest has a feeling of calm and peace.

**Stream**

The mountain stream is crystal clear. At the bottom, rocks in beautiful colors glint in the sun. Small fish dart back and forth, playing in the flowing current. The water is cold and fresh as you splash it on your hands. It flows over rocks with a soothing and gentle babble. The long grass growing at the edge of the stream falls into the water, flowing back and forth with the current. Little water skipper bugs dance on the surface of the water. The warmth of the sun cheers your heart as you bask in this relaxing scene.

**Developing your own "safe" spot.**

For some people, the best place to rest is a mental image of a safe spot that means something to them. A natural place that you really enjoyed alone, when you went to the ocean or the beach, up to the mountains and the trees. Whatever is a place that you enjoy, and you have those positive images and with those images you are thinking about the sights and the sounds and the smells; what it feels like on your skin. A place that gives you a sense of rest. It gives you relief from the stress.

You create the image of a spot in your mind that feels calm and safe to you, a place that you take pleasure in being. Whether it is a city park, neighborhood streets, an ocean or mountains or forest or stream, or whether it is in a room in a building or in a home, it is a place you create for yourself to feel safe and calm. You can step away from whatever is stressing you for a moment and spend a little bit of time in that safe, calm place.

### Making mental images work for you

It takes time and intention to make these lovely images strong and rich enough in your memory so that you can easily access them when you are stressed. However, it's worth the effort so that you can give the memory your full attention and find relief from stress. When you take the time to be aware of and remember the details, the image becomes full and rich in your mind. Later, as you remember the scene, it will give you moments of rest from the day-to-day stress that you experience.

### Selective Focus

The thoughts we think, our patterns of thinking, affect the way we feel. We can add to our uneasiness by thinking troubling thoughts and being in a swirling thinking pattern, thinking about how bad things may get and feeling doomed to escape it. However, the opposite is also true, if we intentionally guide our thoughts we can move towards calmness. Choosing to selectively focus is helping to train our minds in positive and calming habits.

Five-year-old George reclined in the dentist chair, about to have a tooth worked on. The dentist came toward him with a big needle to give him a numbing shot in his gums. George was anxious about it. Then the dentist asked George if he would lift his left foot up a couple of inches and hold it there for a moment. That seemed easy; George was glad to do that. After he raised his foot, the dentist asked him to open his mouth and told him this needle would just pinch a little but keep his foot raised please. The shot was over in two seconds and George handled it just fine.

This pediatric dentist was wise in how he handled giving George a shot. When he asked him to raise his foot, George's focus shifted from the shot he knew was coming to a task he could control: lifting his foot and holding it up. Having his selective focus on his leg, the shot the dentist gave him shifted to the background and therefore was not as troubling. Selective focus is so easy even a five-year-old child can do it.

Try it next time you are at the dentist office. Raise one foot for a little while. It only needs to be a little bit up, but hold it there a moment. What happened to your focus? Your leg muscles get so tense that a lot of your attention was on the muscles in that leg and your focus on willing those muscles to do what you were asked. You can become so distracted by your leg lifting task that you don't pay as much attention to the fact the dentist just jabbed you in the gums with a needle. Selective focus helps us get through tense places.

Have you ever spent time doing something you enjoyed and then you looked up and found hours had passed while you were totally engrossed in that activity? That is a form of selective focus. Your full attention was placed exactly where you wanted it to be. While focused on that aspect, you were ignoring everything else. It can often seem random when that happens. But selective focus is a powerful skill you can intentionally use to make your life better. When you selectively focus on uneasy thoughts, life feels tense. But when you selectively focus on pleasant or fun thoughts, life feels calmer, more productive, and happier. You get to choose what you focus on.

Another form of selective focus is to look at the big picture. To see the task, you are doing in the broader context of your life and the lives of others near and far. To live calmer and feel more at ease by looking for the meaning and purpose of what you are doing. Think about how your task is bringing benefit to yourself, to others and to the world.

Jerry has a very repetitive task at work. He works with a machine that makes the same part over and over. When he takes time to focus on the small details, he notices how well designed the machine is in working with raw materials. There is a pleasing symmetry to the roundness of the part and the motion of the machine. He thinks of his part in this process and how he can make each move count towards more effectiveness. It brings him pleasure to see his skill grow. He enjoys the shine of the metal as the part leaves his workstation.

Henry has a very repetitive task at work. He works with a machine that makes the same part over and over. He constantly is annoyed by this machine. It seems to get jammed up often for no reason. He gets angry and bangs around roughly on it. He thinks about how stupid it is that he has to do this job. He is constantly mad at his bosses, mad at coworkers. Each day he feels stressed and uneasy.

Can you see the difference between the focus of Jerry and Henry? Jerry takes time to understand how the small part he makes fits into the bigger picture of a motor that runs a vehicle. He feels good that he is helping people and materials be able to move from place to place. He feels a sense of pride when he sees vehicles on the roads that contain the type of part he works on. This gives him a sense of purpose, knowing how he is bringing benefit to the world. Henry thinks only of the repetitive motion of his work and how he feels it is dumb. He feels no sense of purpose; he believes he is worthless and has no value, and his work is worthless and has no value. When we understand how what we do affects the lives of others, it can bring a sense of order and purpose to our lives, which contributes to being calm.

Curiosity

Curiosity is an important habit. It lets your mind be active, not passive. Your mind wants to understand things; it wants to actively figure things out. Being curious is having a strong desire to know or learn something, asking questions, and searching for patterns and answers. The mind becomes stronger through exercise. When you use selective focus to be curious, you are exercising your mind.

Curiosity opens up new worlds and possibilities. The world is full of wonders big and small. By being curious, you bring excitement into your life about what you will discover. The curious person is never bored. There are always new things that attract your attention, there are always new 'toys' to play with, new thoughts to think about.

When Janet says, "I'm bored," what she is actually saying is that she has not looked at her surroundings with curious eyes. Curious people see learning as a fun adventure. In school, Janet found learning a burden at times, often being made to learn things she had no interest in. But having curiosity means you are involved in delight-directed study: whatever you delight in, that is what you study. The world is filled with wonders.

It is simple to become more curious. Do not take things for granted. Look to understand why things are like they are. Ask questions of yourself and ask others: Who? What? Where? When? Why? How? What is that? Who made it? When was it made? Why is it that way? Where does it come from? How does it work? How does it interact with other things? Ask yourself: What contributes to the way things are? What would happen if one of those aspects was different? Be open to learn, unlearn, and relearn. Some of the things you know may be wrong, or not fully understood. Learn to be open to those possibilities.

Another way to be curious is to look at small details, to find beauty and enjoyment in the task at hand. There can be something soothing about doing the same task over and over. It is a known event. You can concentrate on making it more effective, moving more toward perfect. Look for symmetry, for balance, in the curves or the shapes or the angles. Observe the colors. Find one element that is enjoyable. Think about the ingenuity of the person who designed the equipment to do this thing.

Choosing to focus on a detail or distraction to lower the intensity of other thoughts, cultivating a sense of curiosity. When you selectively focus on those kinds of things, that awareness helps you take a moment of rest from the stresses of doing the task. You can become calmer. Our minds crave new things, new experiences, something novel and not yet understood. When you use selective focus to be curious about positive or neutral things, you are keeping calm.

Laughter

Finding ways to laugh can lower our stress. Watching funny entertainment that is clean and positive can bring us a burst of pure laughter that gladdens the heart. Watching children play and laugh can bring us laughter. Life is full of funny and ironic moments that will treat us with a laugh.

Laughter is good medicine. Having a good laugh induces physical changes in your body. You take in more air and increase the endorphins releases of your brain. Laughter gives you a good, relaxed feeling. Laughter aids in muscle relaxation which can reduce physical stress. Laughter also improves your immune system and relieves pain. Laughter lightens depression and you can feel happier.

It is good to spend time with positive, clean laughter. Good friends share laughter. A note of caution about laughter; taunting laughter, laughter that makes fun at the expense of others is not helpful and may cause negative effects. I even encourage people to avoid sarcasm. Sarcasm is like lemon juice. In the context of a lot of water and perhaps some sugar it is a refreshing drink. But lemon juice is an acid. Lemon juice in an open cut is painful. Sarcasm done well between good friends can be fun. But sarcasm can also be hurtful and cause others pain.

Laughter with others, the laughter of shared delight takes us out of feelings of unease. Laughter can be one way to face life's difficult situations. Often, we can laugh about troubles that happened in the past, and finding the positive humor in life. If we don't take ourselves too seriously in the past and in the present, we can avoid being distressed by the small stuff. And we may find that most of it is small stuff.

**Skill 2 Managing Your Mind - Mental Images, Selective Focus, Curiosity, and Laughter**

To summarize, skill 2 is managing your mind, which involves intentionally creating and spending time with pleasant images, thoughts, focus and with laughter. When you intentionally manage your mind, you are also influencing the state of your emotions and your body. Building the skill of managing your mind will give you more control over your state of calm or unease.

- Spend time with pleasant mental images of nature.
- Selectively choose to focus on one thing
- Develop more curiosity about the world around you
- Laughter is good medicine

*Remain calm*

*in every situation*

*because peace*

*equals power*

*Joyce Meyer*

# CHAPTER SIX

## Managing Your Thought Habits - Skill 3

The third key skill of being calm is managing your thought habits, which involves assessing your thinking patterns and deciding which habits are moving you toward unease and which ones are moving you toward calm. Then making the changes to move you toward calmer habits of thought.

Habits of Thought

The way we respond to anxiety, stress and worry is partially out of habit. We have responded like this in the past and therefore it is easy for us to respond the same way in the future. Once they are established, following a habit is almost mindless. However, it takes time to build habits.

Think about what it took for you to learn to drive a vehicle, there were a lot of habits that you developed. It takes intentional effort to learn where to put the vehicle on the road, where the side of the road is, your distance from the other vehicles, when to start braking.

All of those are things you spent time learning to do intentionally. Initially, they took a lot of effort to coordinate. Now you probably do them as second nature because you have practiced. It will take some effort to get them started, but habits can serve us well, especially when they are developed deliberately.

We all have habit patterns of behavior and thinking. These began as children, and we have continued to reinforce them as adults. Well-developed habits are functional skills that help us do many things well. Poor habits can keep us trapped in negative patterns that create uneasiness and dysfunction in our lives. The good news is we can choose to change our habits. It will take time to make a change, though, because of how deeply habits are ingrained. It can feel uncomfortable when you first start to change a habit. That is okay. Discomfort can help motivate us to put in the effort to change. When we are trying to change a habit, it helps to not just try to stop a habit, but rather to replace it with something else that is in line with our values.

Another way to think about habits is like a path through a weedy field. There is a solid, well-traveled path that maps the way you are used to thinking about things. It may feel like an easy way because it is familiar, but the weeds and brambles along the way make it stressful. You change that by intentionally making a choice to go a different way. Creating a new path is hard the first time. It takes extra effort. You are going to have to tramp down the thistles and the grass, fighting your way through that new thought path with effort. The second time you go through, it is not quite as hard, and the third time, it gets a little bit easier. Eventually that new path becomes as easy to travel as the old one was. If you stop traveling the old path, the weeds will grow up there and it makes that old path difficult to travel. The new intentional path that you have made becomes the easy path. You just have to put the effort into it to start with and the old path will grow up with weeds and it will not be a path that you want to take, it will not be your habit anymore.

Negative thought habits keep you trapped in a world that feels uneasy. Those thoughts can create extra stress, making work harder, making relationships harder, and in general sapping your energy unnecessarily. However, just like the new path through the field, you can exchange a negative thought pattern for a neutral or positive thought pattern.

Before we get to the steps to do that, let us take a moment to see where these thought habits come from. Thought patterns start in a lot of different places. A lot of them started in the environment in which we grew up. We are influenced by the important people in our lives when we are children. Parents, siblings, neighbors, teachers, classmates, and the things we watched and read all became embedded in our minds. We saw a number of different patterns of thinking right in front of us from the day we were born. We heard whether these people talked about things in a negative, neutral, or positive way, and we took it in. At some point, we noticed the different ways positive, neutral, and negative thoughts affected us, and we chose, however subconsciously, which way we leaned toward. We always have the choice to just go with the flow, which means thinking in the same type of thought patterns that the people around us are thinking. Instead, though, we can choose to reject some of that negativity and make a habit out of more positive thinking.

Positive, neutral, and negative thoughts affect our feelings in different ways. For instance, look at an apple on a table. Someone used to a negative thought pattern might think, “Oh, I don’t like that kind of apple, and it probably has a worm in it too. It is probably too old, and it isn’t going to taste very good.” Someone with a positive thought pattern could think, “Wow, that’s a wonderful apple. I really like the fresh, crisp taste of apples. I bet it is delicious. I cannot wait to try it.” A neutral thought would be, “There is an apple on the table. It is available to be eaten.” When we can approach things as simple as an apple with such different attitudes, it shows you how we can approach every part of life in these vastly different ways. Calm or uneasy is not so much what happens as it is the way we look at what happens. The meaning that we make out of it is that affects how we feel, how we are going to behave, the level of happiness or unease that we have.

Steps to Change

Changing negative thought habits toward positive thought habits takes some effort. The first step is to be aware of the pattern of thinking you already have. Just observe the thoughts you have about a specific topic. Negative thinking patterns can be a hidden source of worry and stress. It may be hard at first to catch those thoughts and define them as negative or positive because it is such a habit and thoughts flow by so fast. To slow it down, you can take a couple of minutes to write down what you think on a topic.

Three experiments to try:

**Experiment one**

The next time you are getting ready to contact a family member or friend.

- First, write down the thoughts running through your head and name any feelings you have. (*This person likes me and enjoys talking with me. I feel happy talking with them.)*
- Second, examine the thoughts and see if they are negative, neutral, or positive. *(Those are all positive thoughts)*
- Third, examine the thoughts for truth. Is it true? As evidenced by what? *(Yes, this is true. As evidenced by how happy they are when I call, and they take time to talk with me.)*

How easy was it to find what you were thinking and feeling about before this call? Then, when you made the call, were the thoughts you had before the call proven to be accurate? This was practice experiment to show you how to find your habitual thoughts and feelings. The next experiment is a little harder.

**Experiment two**

When you are about to make a phone call to a business or governmental authority that you feel uneasy about.

- First, write down the thoughts running through your head and name any feelings you have. (*This person does not want to talk to me. They do not care about me. I will not be able to get what I need. I feel anxious. This is going to be bad.)*
- Second, examine the thoughts and see if they are negative, neutral, or positive. *(Those are all negative thoughts)*
- Third, examine the thoughts for truth. Is it true? As evidenced by what? *(I do not know if these thoughts are true or not. In the past when I have made these kinds of calls they have felt stressful. But, I have no evidence for this call.)*

How easy was it to find what you were thinking and feeling about before this call? This experiment is to help you find your habitual thoughts and feelings. The next experiment is a little harder.

**Experiment three**

Before you are making a phone call to a business or governmental authority that you feel uneasy about, make an intentional choice to change your negative thoughts to positive, or at least neutral thoughts.

- *The people answering the phone want to have a job, and their job is to take my call and talk with me.*
- *Even though they are taking lots of calls and are busy, I am going to assume they want to help me with what I need.*
- *I can help them by being positive, patient and polite, even cheerful so their day will go better.*
- *This call can go well. I have a good chance of getting what I need.*

When you changed your thoughts to positive or neutral how did it change your feelings? When you made the call, which set of thoughts, the negative or the positive or neutral thoughts were proven to be accurate? Do you think your positive thoughts had an effect on the outcome?

Positive thinking habits can have a positive effect on our lives. To grow more positive, we have to start thinking positively. When you observe what you are telling yourself about a situation, stop and ask yourself, "If I were doing this in a positive way, what would I be telling myself about this thing right now?" The level of positivity or negativity that we send out directly affects our level of happiness or unease. If we come to an unfamiliar situation and we are thinking negative things about how bad it is going to be, then we begin to feel more stressed. If we look at this and we talk about the positive aspects, we are generally not nearly as stressed. If we can assess it neutrally, saying, "Well it has some of this and some of that," we can move away from a negative thought spiral as well. The level of calmness we feel is greatly affected by our thoughts.

Another way to grow more positive is to work with a mental health professional. Counseling can help you to work through some of the places where negative thinking habits have developed and can help you to change. Sometimes the negative thinking patterns are so strongly held we do not even notice we are doing it. Your therapist can help you to identify negative or distorted thinking patterns and help you with strategies for how to shift that to neutral or positive.

**Skill 3 Managing Your Thought Habits**

To summarize, skill 3 is managing your thought habits, which involves assessing your thinking patterns and deciding which habits are moving you toward unease and which ones are moving you toward calm. When you intentionally manage and change your thinking patterns you are also influencing your state of calm or unease.

- Assess your thinking patterns.
- Decrease negative thoughts.
- Increase positive and neutral thoughts.

***Sometime in your day today,***

***try to turn off***

***all the noises***

***you can around you,***

***and give yourself***

***some 'quiet time.'***

***In the silence,***

***let yourself***

***think about something.***

***Or if possible,***

***think about nothing.***

***Fred Rogers***

# CHAPTER SEVEN

## Technology and Your Focus - Skill 4

The fourth key skill of being calm is about technology and your focus, which involves paying attention to the kind of information you allow into your mind. Be aware of the effect media has on your sense of unease or calm. Then make changes to the way you interact with media to move you toward being calmer.

Entertained and Informed

Who controls your focus? We are affected by technology in many parts of our lives. Mostly that comes in the form of what media is around you, whether that media is music and other entertainment you watch, listen to, or read, or the passive ways advertising is used to influence, track, and market to you. All of these seek to take your focus and attention. Controlling your limited focus and attention can help keep you calm.

We do need to be exposed to new and enjoyable experiences, whether its children playing with toys, teens or adults watching media, or adults playing games or reading. To regain your focus, you need to keep track of the tone and theme of your entertainment. To use a more extreme example, if all someone watches and reads is horror or similarly fear-themed media, you can expect them to be more fearful and possibly have nightmares related to what entertainment they were consuming. A more calming choice would be to consider more positive entertainment, like watching nature or cooking shows or listening to instrumental music. This isn't to say you have to avoid all negative things, just keep in mind what feelings and reactions they are causing in you. Then consume more positive media than you do negative, or choose to entertain yourself.

Internal and external entertainment

Entertainment comes in two major forms: external entertainment created by others that we view or take part in, and internal entertainment that we create for our own amusement. Media, films, games, and toys are all examples of external entertainment. In this form, we are reliant on devices and on others to create content. The attitude is, "somebody entertain me." Internal entertainment is stuff we make up to entertain ourselves; it does not rely on others for us to have fun.

Janie was totally reliant on external entertainment and when her electronics lose power, she has nothing to play, nothing to watch, nothing to read, and no one else around. Therefore she feels bored, uneasy, and unhappy. She doesn't know what to do with herself.

Mary enjoyed external entertainment, but when power is lost, with nothing to do and nothing to read and no one else around, she looks around and finds ways to entertain herself. She uses her curiosity and imagination to create interesting things to think about and do on her own.

No one else, and no particular situation, can make you bored. Boredom comes from within yourself. Entertainment also can come from within yourself. It is a learned skill. In many parts of history and in many places in the world, this skill is learned in early childhood. But this skill has been slow to develop when there has been a strong reliance on external technology and entertainment, as there has been in recent history. Mary has a calmer life because she doesn't have to worry about losing power to her devices. She always has the ability to calm herself and be entertained. She is less inclined to listen to low-quality media or news sources.

The media you interact with can be negative or positive. Negative stories will keep your attention better, as the reaction will be stronger and therefore be remembered longer. A newspaper once conducted an experiment where they only published good or positive news stories for a day. They lost 2/3 of their readers for that day. (Epstein, 2014).

Negative stories can cause a negative reinforcement loop, where you keep looking for more exciting content, distracting you from what you planned to be doing. The negative effects linger even after you go back to whatever you had planned. There are alternatives to this negative feedback loop.

This same negative and positive cycle needs to also be applied to the news, as they are the masters of using negatively focused stories to keep your attention on them. You as the reader, watcher, or listener should be noticing tone and actively look for positive stories, even if you have to look elsewhere. It is good to listen to a balance of views, so we have a wider perspective of the world. By doing this first step, you can prevent a persistent uneasy mindset in reaction to seeing negative news. Yes, negative or shocking events happen every day. But they are not all that goes on in the world and not all of them need our attention. Ads in various forms affect you, perhaps subtly, even if you do not think they do. If it did not work, why would companies pay to make sure people see their ads repeatedly?

To regain your focus and keep yourself calm involves three steps.

1. Pay attention to what keeps you entertained or up to date with current events and what its tone is.

2. Be aware of and reduce what passively eats up your attention.
3. Finally, take a step back away from technology every so often.

Passive Attention

When we passively allow our attention to drawn by media output, we are allowing outside influences to affect the way we feel, think, or behave. That form of passive influencing is why advertising exists and works so well. You may be wondering how this relates to being calm. The less you allow these ads to subtly shape your views, emotions, behaviors, and actions the calmer and more in control of your life you can be. This advertising is designed to create a dissatisfaction in you, to create a need—for their product or service. This can add to a feeling of unease. You can limit your exposure to some of this marketing by using ad-blocking technology to filter out some of the "shocking" ads that pose as articles or news at the bottom of webpages and the targeted ads that show up after you talked about something or looked at something online. Given that some forms of those ads are not just plain text on a page but full of distracting sights, sounds, and colors, it makes for a calmer browsing experience for multiple reasons.

The passive attention hijacking isn't just happening online though. Notifications on multiple devices also are designed to grab your attention. Think of them as a mini billboard yelling "HEY LOOK

AT ME, NOW!!!" If they aren't the notifications you intentionally allow for people, places, or events you want to be notified of immediately, then it is an interruption of your focus. There are more active ways to use technology to manage how both the notifications and media affect you.

Take a Step Back

This skill can be done in various forms; most of them are active. First, there is being outside. Multiple studies have shown (Gladwell et al., (2013)) being outside frequently to be better for one's mental health, even without exercising. Sitting outside can be made even more calming by journaling with a pen and paper, or with meditation. Your mind is always in motion, but you can calm it by directing your focus. Getting moving will help calm your mind by diverting some of its focus to keeping you spatially aware of what is around you.

Another calming use of technology is using your devices to listen to positive music and audiobooks. Fitness apps can measure and track your level of calm, allowing you to grow in your ability to gain more physical and mental calmness. For example, various apps exist to guide you through both deep breathing and meditation. These and other positive technologies used in moderation can help you keep both your attention and your smart devices under your control.

See our website for more lists of positive technology and how to use them.

FREE resource guides for taking active control of your technology and focus can be found at:

**www.faithfulhabits.com/keepingcalm**

Being Calm in a World of Technology

What technology can help me be calmer? There are many answers to this. The first question to answer is do you want to directly be assisted in being calm?

- Timers, reminders or follow-along prompts for meditation, deep breathing, or prayer are examples of this.
- Reminders or scheduled limits of how long of a block of time you spend in distracting apps or devices, usually by only giving you a set amount of time or only letting them be used at certain times of day, are examples of this kind of assistance.
- Another option is to get reminded to go and do something else, be it just getting up and walking around every twenty minutes.
- While using your technology, setting a goal of completing a step in a project or task and rewarding yourself by going away from it and thinking of something else for a while.

Studies (J, Zheng P, Jia Y, Chen H, Mao Y, Chen S, et al. (2020)) have shown using social media can worsen or incite depression or other negative emotions or negatively affect your mental health, usually by creating a negative feedback loop that relies on your emotions being triggered toward more of that content. The now-ancient phrase "If it bleeds it leads" regarding newspapers works the same for what is written online. They also use the aforementioned attention-grabbing techniques to keep you glued there.

You can use reminders and tracking tools to help you form helpful habits. Some examples are getting used to stepping away from your various screens thirty minutes to an hour before you sleep and spending that time using pencil and paper, writing out what you are currently feeling and how you think you got there. There are studies (Woods, H.C., Scott, H. (2019)) that show being away from your devices for an hour before bed can give you better quality sleep.

Modern technology should be a supporting element, like a plate, something that is supposed to be there to help you, not have you only help it. How that interaction goes and for how long can be something you have a level of control over. A delightful life is possible without electronics; they are simply a helpful tool for us to use. Knowing you can shape your technology use frees you from being owned by the electronics. Understanding that you can entertain yourself without electronics can be calming.

To summarize, the fourth key skill of being calm is about technology usage and your focus, which involves paying attention to the kind of media you allow into your mind. Be aware of the effect media tone has on your sense of unease or sense of calm. Then make changes to the way you interact with technology to move you toward being calmer.

**Skill 4 Technology and Your Focus**

- Be aware of how you are being entertained and informed.
- Look at where your passive attention is focused.
- Step away from technology periodically, give yourself a breather.

Use technology to help you focus on a calmer life.

*Keep calm*

*and carry on.*

*Winston Churchill*

*I will be calm.*

*I will be mistress*

*of myself*

*Jane Austen*

# CHAPTER EIGHT

## Manage Your Attitude - Skill 5

The fifth key skill of being calm is managing your attitude. The way we approach life, our attitude greatly affects our feeling of calmness or uneasiness. Defining what we can change and what we need to adapt to or accept is vital. The attitude of acceptance and gratefulness is a key to contentment, which is the realization of how much you already have.

Acceptance

*God, grant me the serenity*
*to accept the things I cannot change,*
*courage to change the things I can,*
*and wisdom to know the difference.*

*Reinhold Niebuhr*

The changeables in our lives are the things that we can make choices about. We can change the way we look at the world. We can change our values and beliefs, the things we deem important. What we cannot change, we can choose to adapt to or choose to just accept. We cannot change other people, but we can choose how we will interact with them. We need to accept how this person is and make our choices determined on that rather than waiting for them to change. What we can think about is our responsibility and what is not our responsibility. You have a choice in how you respond to situations and your attitude. You do not have to make decisions about or worry about problems that are not yours. When you try to look at the whole picture, including decisions other people make, and take on responsibility for everything, it can be overwhelming. It can cause a lot of unease, a lot of anxiety. When we let go of anything we have no control over, it can be calming. Then we are free to focus on what we can change.

Some people find getting motivated to change difficult, they think it is too hard to change, that it will take too much effort. It is true that changing will take effort. Let us frame it another way. Say it takes 10 units of effort in order to change a habit, but once I have created the new habit, doing the task will only take 2 units of effort. I do not want to put in the 10 units of effort, so I keep doing the task like it is now. The trouble is the way I am doing it now takes 4 units of effort every time I complete it. If I do that task five times a week, I am wasting 10 units of effort weekly.

For example, the latch on Joe's backyard gate sticks. Every time he has to go through it, he has to fiddle with that sticky latch. It takes him an extra 15 seconds and a little frustration to deal with it 12 times a week. He spends 3 minutes a week in uneasiness and frustration over that sticky gate latch. That is 2.5 hours per year. How long would it take to fix that latch? Maybe about an hour, including the run to a hardware store. If Joe would put in the effort to take an hour to fix the latch, he would save himself an extra hour and a half in the first year. Over 5 years, he has saved over 12.5 hours. From then on, there is no frustration in going through that gate. It becomes an automatic thing that fades into the background and Joe can concentrate on why he is going through the gate, not the fact that the gate itself is frustrating to get through.

So, which one of those paths actually takes more effort: To fix the gate or to keep working with it the way it is? Are you motivated by not having to work as hard? Motivation to change comes in many ways and forms. What may motivate me may not motivate you, but a lot of motivational aspects are universal. For example, the road towards home often seems easier or shorter than the road to work. This effect is because on the road home we are anticipating that we will have family, food and rest, now that our day is over and in thinking of that we are not as bothered by the slight annoyances of the journey.

When Sandy was a child, she had the task of hoeing weeds on the farm corn patch. Hoeing a really long row of corn seemed like a huge task. It was tiring just to look at how much was in front of her to do. She would look behind to see how much she had already done. What Sandy discovered is that when she had passed halfway, she began to get motivated to work hard to finish because now there was less in front of her than there was behind her. She could tell herself that the hardest part was over. She was nearly done and now all she had to do was the finishing up. That became one of Sandy's habits of how to deal with all sorts of difficult projects.

Sandy would think about the end goal of what she wanted to accomplish. She took time to get a clear mental image of the result. How nice it would be to have that goal. Then she broke the goal into little steps. She would start a step and tell herself, "All I have to do is this next little step. Just do the next little step, and then the next little step." As she moved forward, she kept encouraging herself that all she had to do is this next piece. She would not look at the whole task, just doing the next piece. Eventually, she would get to where she was over halfway done. That realization gave her the thrill that felt like she was nearly finished. What was behind her was bigger than what was in front of her. Therefore, she found the motivation to run to the finish because she was nearly done.

Jerry feels like he is too lazy to change. But when he thinks about it, he realizes the lazy person is the person who wants to do things in the most efficient way possible. They spend the least time possible doing it, so in reality the lazy person is the one who does things effectively. Like with the sticky gate: You might think a lazy person does not want to fix the gate, but actually, the lazy person is the one who will fix the gate, because they do not want to have to constantly put the effort into working with that sticky thing all the time.

In this story we have reframed what it means to be lazy. Tell your lazy self the easiest way to put in the least effort is to put a little more effort in the beginning. Jerry encourages himself by saying, “Okay, I like being lazy, but the best way to be lazy is to get things done so I do not have to deal with constant frustration.”

Madison feels too afraid to change. She feels she is getting by okay the way she is. She is scared that changing will put her in painful places. The unknown of something different makes her feel anxious that maybe people will not like her if she changes.

Let us look at those fears a little closer. Sometimes the discomfort that we know—that we are familiar with—seems too hard to change to something new. Because something new is unfamiliar, we might label it as uncomfortable, but uncomfortable is not the same as unfamiliar. When we make changes, it is always going to feel unfamiliar for a little while. When we get used to the new way, then it becomes familiar and even comfortable. Accept going in it is going to feel different and awkward, but that difference and awkwardness is not necessarily uncomfortable; it is just unfamiliar. Sometimes we hang on to old, painful stuff because the pain we know seems better than the unknown of what it would be if we changed. But it is well worth becoming familiar with not having pain.

Try that thumb-on-top experiment again, thinking about the comfort of change. Put your two hands together with your fingers interlaced. Now do it again faster. Now make a small change. Put your hands together again, but this time with the other thumb on top. Notice how it feels to have the other thumb on top. If you are like most people, it feels awkward and unfamiliar. Notice that although it feels unfamiliar, it is not actually uncomfortable. Sometimes the feeling we label as "uncomfortable" is actually just "unfamiliar." The way we move the unfamiliar to the familiar is by repeating the experience until we are thoroughly familiar with the new experience. From there, a little more effort can move something from familiar to a habit. If you were to continue to intentionally put the other thumb on top, you would be moving toward changing that habit.

For some people, having a sense of unease has become their identity. "That person is the pretty one, that person is strong, and I am the nervous one who is always uneasy. If I am not the nervous one, who am I?"

You are a person of value. You are a person who has abilities and strengths and can change. You can change your reputation. You can change your identity to what you want. You have the power to do that.

How do we decide what are the changeable things or the unchangeable things in life? Write out a list and describe the characteristics of each item to yourself. Ask trusted friends and advisors and counselors: is this something I need to accept or is this something that can be changed? Ask a multitude of advisors, not just one. Then compare their answers and then write out to yourself what would it look like if you change this. What would it look like if you keep trying to change it? What would it look like if you accepted it for what it was and learned to make your choices of what you're going to do knowing that this is what it is going to be and then you adapt to what is?

For example, I am a woman who is 5 foot 9 inches /175 cm tall. I have a large bone structure. If I do not want to accept that I have a large bone structure, if I rail against largeness, is that going to make me petite? No. I can try all kinds of things to give an illusion of being petite, but that won't make me petite. Instead, when I behave out of context with reality, what I have become is somebody whose judgment other people might question. Why not just accept who I am and find what is good in that? If I want to stay stuck in a problem, I can stay stuck in a problem. That is my choice. But staying stuck is an uneasy place to be.

I can choose to accept what I cannot change. I have looked at it, I have examined the different ways it can be handled, and if I choose that acceptance is the right choice, I make that decision. The important next step is to stop deciding. I do not ask myself everyday if I am going to accept this. I just do it. It is like accepting the weather. If I spend my energy railing against the rain, the rain is not going to go away. I will just feel frustrated. If I accept that it rains, then I will wear protective rain gear to keep me comfortable. I adapt to it, and it does not take any energy; it is neutral. Acceptance is an important part of moving toward a calmer life.

### Gratefulness

If you think about the last vehicle you got, the weeks before you chose that make and model and color, how many of those vehicle types did you see on the road? If you are like most of us, you did not pay much attention to it before you started thinking it was a vehicle you wanted. But the day after you buy that vehicle, how many of them did you see on the road? Likely, you began to see them everywhere, at every intersection. Does that mean there were more of those vehicles on the road than there were before? No. What it means is that after you bought one you were keyed in to look for that make and model. You have identified that this item or subject or thing as important; therefore, you will recognize it everywhere.

It is the same about seeing the good in life around you. If you think the world is good, you see evidence of good all around you. If you think the world is bad, then you have a tendency to see bad everywhere, because you are keyed in to look for bad, chaos, and disaster. If you seek to see things that are not right, you will see lots of things that produce feelings of unease. The truth is, there are lots of things in the world that are troubling. But that is not all there is in the world. If we just look at the troubling things, we will feel uneasy a lot of the time.

However, there are a lot of good, positive things in the world and if we seek to see those things, we will feel calmer. When we seek to see what is true, noble, and right, we will feel calmer. When we intently look for what is pure, things that are lovely, and the beauty around us, feelings of unease fade away. When we search for what is excellent and character traits that are admirable or praiseworthy, we are encouraged. We are more hopeful and have more calm.

When you focus only on the bad, you get uneasy. Anxiety and stress build. When you focus on the good around you, it does not mean you do not see the bad. You cannot help seeing it. But when you recognize there is a lot of good in the world too, you feel calmer, more at ease, and more at rest.

Sally feels like the world owes her a living, like everything should be handed to her. She feels like a victim of life's circumstances and therefore everybody should do stuff for her. That sense of entitlement also makes her feel like nothing is ever good enough. No matter what anyone does for her, she feels unsatisfied. She wants something else and more stuff. Sally finds it hard to keep friends. They drift away from her as she becomes more demanding. Sally feels sad and lonely, always uneasy, and unfulfilled. It is a difficult life for her.

Maria is an easy person to be around. She expects to work for what she gets. She is grateful for everything she has. When someone does something for her, she tells them how happy she is about it. Every time you see Maria, she will ask about your life and tell you about the wonderful things that happened to her. Her life seems to be filled with things that she is thankful for. Her life is calm and happy.

Life is uncertain and life is hard. How can you be grateful when you are in the middle of hard circumstances? It is about recognizing that contentment is not the fulfillment of what you want. Contentment is the realization of how much you already have.

When Charlotte is asked how she is, she always answers "Fabulous!" When asked to explain why she is doing fabulous, she tells people, "Today I was able to get up by myself. I feed myself. I dress myself. I can ask for what I want. I am doing fabulous!" Charlotte recognizes that these are things to be grateful for because she drives a school bus for those who cannot do those things for themselves.

If we take the time to look, we will see that even when we are in hard circumstances, there are good things all around us. You can see the good things if you are keyed to look for them. Life feels calmer when you are grateful for what you have.

Finding Beauty

Finding beauty is another one of the calming skills. As humans we are created to recognize beauty and respond to beauty. It is another form of selective focus. Everywhere around us is beauty. In nature, the colors of green on the trees and the plants vary from tree to tree, leaf to leaf. Some trees are yellow or gold; some are a dark purple red color. There is tremendous diversity in leaf shapes, and they are all beautiful. Some leaves are big and wide. Some are narrow and thin, some are tiny stubs, and some are almost round. All these leaves dance and flutter in the wind differently. All of that is beautiful. When we focus on the wonder of beauty our attitude may move naturally to a gratefulness that the beauty is there and that we get to enjoy it.

Look at the faces of people. Each one is different; each one is beautiful in its own way. Look at the beauty in their eyes, not just the beauty of the color, but also beauty of expression and character. We humans are created with tremendous diversity and all of it beautiful.

There is a beauty in architecture, the way a building is designed, not just to keep out the weather. Buildings are designed with symmetry and grace, and there is a beauty in their functionality. Notice the pleasing harmony of the way that the materials are put together, the paint, the trim, windows, and the rooflines. In some buildings, it is obvious that someone found joy in creating that design.

Take a close look at fabrics, their weaves and the textures. Fabrics are also about color and the pattern. The way patterns repeat on fabric is amazing. These are just a few examples of beauty all around you. Looking at beauty gives your eyes something pleasant to look at it, gives your brain something pleasant to admire. Beauty is everywhere. Recognizing the beauty and being grateful for it is calming.

**Skill 5 Manage Your Attitude**

To summarize, the fifth key skill of being calm is managing your attitude. The way we approach life, our attitude greatly affects our feeling of calmness or uneasiness. The attitude of acceptance and gratefulness is important to contentment, which is the calm realization of how much you already have.

- Practice acceptance.
- Increase your gratefulness.
- Look for the beauty around you.

*The pursuit,*

*even of the best things,*

*ought to be calm and tranquil.*

*Cicero*

*On average,*

*the deeper people's*

*knowledge of a topic,*

*the more calmly*

*they talk about it*

*Paul Graham*

# CHAPTER NINE

## Managing Core Values - Skill 6

The sixth key skill is about managing core values, which includes learning to have integrity, the calmness of doing the right thing. Also, when life has stressful, difficult circumstances, learning to seek out the good that can come from challenging times. And finally, practicing compassion for self and others,

Integrity

Integrity is one of the key skills to being calm. When you are living life in line with your values, you have integrity. Integrity has three definitions. 1) To have integrity is to be true and honest, someone we can depend on. 2) To have integrity is to be integrated. What we are on the inside, we are on the outside. What we are like with our friends, we are like at the workplace. What we are on Friday night, we are on Sunday morning. Everything about us, our values, and the way we treat people is integrated into every part of our life. 3) To have integrity means to be whole and complete and fit for purpose. For example, we would say that a water bottle has integrity if it does not leak. It is whole and complete and fit for its purpose.

Integrity gives us a road map of how to make our decisions. It helps us sort through the choices that we need to make so we are not anxious. We can feel calmly confident that we are going to make choices with integrity in line with our own values.

Integrity does not just appear on its own. Integrity is a character trait we need to see modeled. When we learn to recognize it around us, we can grow that character trait within ourselves. Integrity means that we do the right thing even when nobody is looking.

We grow integrity in all the little choices that do not seem to matter. An example, by not cheating at board games. When we do what is right in all the little ways, it is easier for us to do what is right in the bigger ways. For example, a person with integrity would not read another person's diary, even if it were left open and unguarded. A person with integrity recognizes that is somebody else's information, and it is not ours and therefore we are going to respect it even if nobody would ever know whether we had read it. We would know. What we do when nobody but ourselves can find out either builds our character or erodes our character. These are choices that we make every day.

Having strong internal character helps us to be calm. When we are not being swayed by opinions and we have taken the time to think out our values, it gives us a solid template to make decisions. We get in the habit of making the right decisions. Right decisions are a hallmark of a calmer life.

Finding Good

Spreading good is to act justly, treating others in a way that acknowledges their value, to give grace and be merciful with others and to walk humbly. The world is a calmer place, and it makes life much more at ease for everyone, when you spread good.

If you try, you can see the good in even in bad circumstances. When something is bad, it is generally not all bad. There is still something good that can come out of it. When Mount Saint Helens, erupted that volcanic blast devastated more than 200 square miles. That was bad. The volcanic ash spread around the world within two weeks. Volcanic ash makes an excellent fertilizer. There was a lot of destruction at the base of the mountain—that is true. But further away from the blast, more nutrients were added to the soil, making it produce better crops. The circle of good was tremendously bigger than the circle of bad. In the areas that were devastated by that eruption, people thought it might take a hundred years for flora and fauna to return. Scientists were surprised that little bits of life were evident even in that first year. Plants started growing within a year after the blast. Animals returned, plants grew again, so that now, decades after the blast, it is a rich and diversified environment. Different than it was in many ways, but beautiful.

Very few people are truly bad. There is evil in the world and some people have embraced it. However, in most people, the good and the bad are mixed. They make good choices, and they make bad choices. Most of us have made bad choices many times. When we made a bad choice, it may have affected other people. For example, if we decide to dash through that yellow traffic light hoping we can get to where we are going a little bit faster, we may cause somebody else to have to stop suddenly so they can avoid an accident. Perhaps there was no accident this time, but it caused them an uneasy feeling; it made their world feel a little bit less safe.

Since all of us make bad choices now and then, we could show mercy to others, knowing that many times we have been shown mercy. We can give grace and undeserved favor because all of us need it. We can treat others like we want to be treated. When we treat others respectfully with a calm attitude it is more likely that we will be treated in the same way.

If you seek goodness, you will find it, because you find what you look for. A story is told of an old farmer working in his front field by the main road that went through his town. Some people drove up and a woman asked him what his town was like, what the people were like. She said her family was looking for a place to move to and wondered what the people were like here. The old farmer asked what the people were like where she came from. She replied, they were awful. Selfish and always fussing about stuff and fighting and making trouble and grasping for things that weren't theirs. The old farmer looked at her and said, "You know, people are just like that here." She drove away.

Another vehicle came up and another woman asked the old farmer, "We have to move to a new area, and I was wondering what the people are like here." Again, the old farmer asked this woman, "What were the people like in the last place you lived?" She said, "They were the nicest people. It just broke our hearts to leave there. Everybody was so kind and gracious." The old farmer replied, "You know, people are just like that here."

That old farmer gave an accurate answer to both people, because what you look for you find, and what you give out is what you are going to get back. If you behave selfishly and are argumentative, you are going to find the people around you are selfish and argumentative. But if your behavior focuses on calmly displaying kindness and goodness, you will find that there is a lot of kindness and goodness in the world. If you seek goodness, you will find it.

Understand that we are rich if we have more food to eat than we need today and shelter that covers more than just our own body. We are rich if we have more clothes than what we are wearing. We are rich if we have friends and family who care about us. We are rich, and out of that abundance we can share with others. Generosity and giving out of a grateful heart bring peace and happiness to us.

Another example of finding good in difficult places is the periodic wildfires. The Giant Sequoia needs fire to help it to reproduce. It is not alone in that need. There are other pines and other plants which depend on fire to help their seeds be viable. Fire is a stressful and destructive process in a forest, and yet good comes from it as well.

When we are in a stressful and destructive season of life, we need to be open to the way that good may also come from this troubling time. It may not be the good we expect. It may not be what we had before, but goodness can win out.

Compassion

It is not about you. It is not about you! The world is bigger than you know and all of us live here together. It is worth looking at the larger context of the world and just what you want this moment. We can get to thinking the world is all about us, but it is not. In nature, living things work together. In the garden, there are plants that, when they grow next to certain others, benefit from the proximity. For example, clover is a nitrogen fixing plant that helps to nourish plants that are nearby. There are trees that grow tall and reach for the sky. Other trees and plants and bushes need the shade provided by those trees.

We too need other people in our lives. We support them; they support us. We are designed to be in community. We flourish in community. Some people need to connect deeply with just a few others and some people need to connect broadly with a lot of others. Left to ourselves we can grow lopsided in how we respond to stress, when we reach out to others, supporting and being supported it helps us all live calmer lives and be more balanced.

One of the simple ways to show our interconnectedness is to put that in money terms. I need to pay her, so she can pay him, so he can pay them, so they can pay those others, and those others can pay you, and you pay me. We are all interconnected. Similarly, when we help others to be calmer, it makes us happy, and we are more likely to be calm within ourselves.

Another aspect that helps us be calmer is looking at life with compassionate curiosity is wondering how life is for others: the jobs they do, and the problems they might be facing. From there, we have compassion for them. When we care about people and what their needs are, we are less focused on our own feelings. I see the world from my point of view all the time. But when I move out of that focus and think about what the world looks like from the point of view of another person, it broadens my understanding of the world. A simple way to do this is to ask yourself, "What does this place look like from the point of view of the person opposite me?" Imagine what they see that is blocked from your angle. What do you see that is blocked from their angle? Then go over that side and look at it to see how accurate you were. We will never know exactly what their view is because we do not have their exact level of vision, knowledge, and experience. But we can try to understand a great deal of it. When we seek to understand another person's point of view, our world opens up a little wider, becomes a little richer. We can become more compassionate when we understand more.

Compassionate curiosity is another way to have more calm in our lives. A good exercise is to think about what life is like for somebody else. This is where we use our imagination, informed by our knowledge and experience. For example, think about a child that is two or three years old. Put yourself for a moment at the height of that child, what does the world look like from that angle? What hazards do you see? What comforts do you see? What are the resources that are available? What are the things that are out of reach? How do you get a drink of water? When we think about what life is like for somebody else it, makes us gentler and kinder people.

When you are feeling uneasy and you are around others who are feeling uneasy, you can calm yourself by moving out of your focus to compassion. What do these other people need? Is there any way that you could encourage or comfort or provide them something they need to feel calmer? While we are thinking about what they need, we stop focusing on our own sense of uneasiness and we become calmer. When we help them be calmer and the calmness we need, we help them to find will also begin to fill us. When we pay attention to what others may need and help them, we are giving them hope and it reflects hope back onto us.

Think about this old parable about what heaven and hell are like. Hell is described as a room with a large pot of delicious stew. The people there each have a long-handled spoon, too long to reach their own mouth. They are starving and miserable. Heaven is like a room that looked just the same, with a large pot of delicious stew. The people each have a long-handled spoon, too long to reach their own mouth. They are well-fed and happy. What is the difference? In the second room, the people feed each other, and everyone has as much as they want. In the first room people are selfishly only thinking of their own needs, and they are starving. When we help others with their needs, we can also get our own needs met.

**Skill 6 Managing Core Values**.

In summary skill six is about managing core values which includes learning to have integrity, the calmness of doing the right thing. Also, when life has stressful, difficult circumstances, learning to seek out the good that can come from challenging times. And practicing compassion for self and others.

- Increase the integrity in your life.
- Seek out and finding the good in the world.
- Practice compassion for yourself and for others.

***Someone's sitting***

***in the shade today***

***because someone***

***planted a tree***

***a long time ago.***

***Warren Buffett***

# CHAPTER TEN

## Prevention and Planning - Skill 7

The seventh and final skill of this book is prevention and planning. There are ways you can set up your life to avoid foreseeable problems. Assessing the things that cause unease in your life and doing a risk assessment on them. - How likely is it, and how bad would it be. The very act of assessing risk, and planning how to face it leaves us feeling more confident and therefore calmer.

*Plans are worthless, but planning is everything. There is a very great distinction because when you are planning for an emergency you must start with this one thing: the very definition of "emergency" is that it is unexpected, therefore it is not going to happen the way you are planning. The details of a plan which was designed years in advance are often incorrect, but the planning process demands the thorough exploration of options and contingences. The knowledge gained during this probing is crucial to the selection of appropriate actions as future events unfold.*

*Dwight Eisenhower*

Planning is a way to calmer living that prevents some of the common things that stir us up into a life of unease. A piece of good news, a lot of the chaos in our lives is of our own making. That means you can change those things to make your life calmer.

Charles has a job he likes, but he gets stressed out, worrying that he will get fired. That stress affects his performance. He loses sleep over it and therefore goes into work tired and does not do his job at the quality he wants to. Finally, Charles decides he has enough of this uneasiness in his life, so he asks himself, "So what? If I lost this job, what would I do?" He takes the time to update his resume, gather the names of other companies he would like to work for, and write out a plan of what he would do the day after he would no longer have this job. Then he files that all away. Now, when his brain wants to feel uneasy about potentially losing his current job, he can remind himself that it would be uncomfortable, but he has a valid plan of what to do next, so it is nothing to worry about. Now he sleeps better and arrives at work refreshed and generally ready to do the quality of work he is capable of.

By facing his fear and making a plan of how to move forward if he lost his job, Charles has moved into a calmer life and is also less likely to lose his job.

Planning is about facing your fears and not letting them trap you into a life of unease.

Prevention is easier than repair. For example, we wear seatbelts in a car to help prevent catastrophic injuries. It is easier to prevent harm than it is to heal from it. Risk assessment is about how likely it is something bad will happen and how bad could it be. On any given day, the risk of you being in a motor vehicle accident is low. How bad could it be, though? Catastrophic. So, we wear seatbelts all the time.

*It is better to try to keep a bad thing from happening, than it is to fix the bad thing once it has happened.*

When you look at the worst-case scenario, one of the best things you can do is figure out how to survive it. For example, if your income dropped, how would you live? Do you have money in savings? Mary was surprised how much of her uneasiness faded away when she finally had one month's worth of savings. It has taken effort to save a little bit each month. She decided there were a couple of things in her discretionary spending that she could cut back on. She set up an automatic transfer to savings of a small amount each month. Surprisingly, she did not miss that small amount; she did not even think about it since it automatically happened. Some months later, when she saw how much the amount of her savings had grown, she was grateful, and more calm moved into her life. She had more confidence and she felt happier.

If your life were totally changed, if you could not do the work that you are doing now—physically or because there were no longer jobs in that field, or they weren't economically available—what could you do? What choices would you have? You are more than this job. Your identity is more than this line of work. When you brainstorm, thinking out those choices, you become calmer.

Prevention is looking ahead seeing what could happen and preparing what you could do to keep the worst from happening. Ben is a long-haul truck driver with a very safe driving record. He is always looking ahead on the road, watching ever-changing traffic conditions. He is aware of what the vehicles around him are doing and it is his habit to plan the safety path based on their actions. He constantly makes preventive plans in his head for safe driving in any situation. So, when an emergency comes up, he does not even have to think about what to do. His brain simply pulls up the best template and automatically follows through. This preventive thinking is what helps Ben calmly have a good safety record.

This calm habit of prevention is not about worrying. Prevention is about objectively thinking: if this happened, what could I do? You make a template in your head for how you would survive, planning how you would move forward. A key skill here is to stop. Once you have identified the concern, planned how to prevent it, or survive it to move forward, then you stop thinking about it. Easier said than done. But let us look at a way to begin this process.

Ten-minute exercise.

Set yourself a timer. Within the allotted ten minutes make four quick lists.

1. You identify the concern. Be as thorough as quickly possible, look at a number of layers, without having to have all the layers make sense together at this point. Fully write out an objective view of the concern.

    ➢ *For example: My car may break down. I would not be able to drive. I would not be able to get to work. I could lose my job.*

2. Then write out the emotional aspect of the concern. All the swirling feelings you have about it. Do not require your feeling to make sense at this point, just record what they are.

    ➢ *I would feel scared. I would feel like a loser. I would feel ashamed.*

3. List out the resources you have to bring to this concern. Include things like time, skills, other people, and the ability to research.

    ➢ *I have friends or family that may be able to give me a ride to work. I know a good mechanic. My car is working right now, so I can do regular maintenance to help keep it working. I am able to ride public transportation. I can plan out the public transportation route and how to get tickets needed and how long the trip would take. I could ask family and friends ahead of time that if my car ever stopped working would they be willing to take me to work.*

4. Write out your desired result. Best case scenario, what do you want?

   - *I want to be able to get to work. I want my car to be dependable and keep running so I should keep up with regular maintenance.*

If you have time left over fill gaps on the four items.

Now set it all aside and leave it alone for some hours or even a day or so. Then come back to it and do another ten minutes to clarify the list and add to each section. Again, set it aside and leave it alone for some hours or a day or two. Then you can come back to it and study what you have written and write out a plan to move forward toward your goals.

What has happened in the ten-minute blocks is that you have begun to bring order to chaos. The swirling thoughts in your brain were written out into a more ordered form. When you did the second ten-minute exercise, you brought even more order to the thoughts. In the times between focusing on the concern, your brain has been busy in the background working on understanding it more and figuring out how to move forward. No longer stuck trying to remember all the pieces and layers, since they were written down, you were able to make progress.

Lydia and Grace each plan to stop on the way home from work to get a few needed groceries. Lydia repeats her list to herself a few times during the day: milk, eggs, and bread. She repeats it again as she leaves work, and while driving to the store. She is a little uneasy, not wanting to forget anything. Lydia gets into the store with all the distractions and comes home with five items, but no bread.

Grace writes out her list first thing and puts it in her pocket. Milk, eggs, and bread. All day she focuses on what is in front of her to do. After work, she stops at the store, pulls out her list, gets the three items she needed, and is free to look at a few other things.

Lydia had uneasy moments in her day, worrying about forgetting, and did forget an important item. Grace had a calm day, with a calm shopping trip, and got everything she needed.

Prevention and planning can move a lot more calm into your world. Planning how to handle a troubling concern and writing it out allows your mind to put it to rest. Once you write down your shopping list, you do not have to think about it anymore because you have done what is needed to take care of it. Now your mind can be calm and at peace about it. That also works for big concerns and worries.

Worrying about the present or the future makes us constantly feel uneasy. Our mind thinks of all the bad that might happen, and it becomes a constant swirl of uneasy thoughts and emotions that cannot seem to move forward. It keeps us stuck in an uncomfortable view of a possible negative future, unable to calmly enjoy the present.

Overly optimistic thinking is similar, except we think of unrealistic things we want to have happen. Our mind becomes stuck in a swirl of the glorious possibilities but does not do anything to move forward. It keeps us stuck in an idealistic view of a possible future, unable to calmly enjoy the present.

Plan B

The good Plan B is one that is achievable, measurable, and works with the realistic part of resources you have available to you. It becomes a good option. Maybe not your most favorite option—it is after all it is a Plan B not Plan A—but something that is viable. Additionally, sometimes it can fun to figure out what a Plan C, or D, or E would look like. What if you went into a totally different line of work? What would it take to succeed in that? What training would you need? What kind of places would you work? What would your daily life be like? Would it be inside or outside? Would it be working with people or working alone? It can be fun to just explore that mental image. Write out a plan for it and let your mind play with the idea.

What if thinking about Plan B makes you feel too uneasy? Then give yourself a ten-minute exercise of writing out a Plan B. It is okay to feel uneasy during the ten-minute exercise since you know it will be end and you can do something unfamiliar for ten minutes. Set a timer and when it goes off you are done. Walk away and do something else, something fun. Later, go back and spend another ten minutes. Again, walk away. It can also be helpful to chat with some safe and wise friends about it. Let them know it is just a thinking exercise. That said, your coworkers are not the best source to talk to, because not everybody keeps the things you say to themselves, and it may not be wise to have your boss know that you are thinking about a Plan B.

If you are having trouble thinking of a Plan B, perhaps look at just a little change. If you are working for a company making blue widgets, maybe Plan B is working for a company that makes yellow widgets. Or a company that makes dyes for blue widgets. Sometimes Plan B is just a little bit of a change. You could also consider another department in the same company, or a different shift in the same department. The purpose of a Plan B is to let your mind be calmer, and to not panic over thoughts of losing Plan A.

Sometimes Plan B may sound better than Plan A. That is something to think about in more depth. First, have you accounted for all the logistics of Plan B? Make sure you are looking at it realistically. Are you looking at the difficulties that are involved in Plan B as well as the possible benefits? It can be good to find out you have more options in life. Maybe you will make Plan B into your Plan A.

It might be that Plan B will not work. Or it will not give you exactly what Plan A does. You might have to adjust your lifestyle. You might have to move locations. You might have to work a different shift. None of those things may be desirable to you. But it may still be a good emergency backup plan.

The purpose of the Plan B exercise is to calm the uneasy feeling that if you lose your Plan A job you will be sleeping under a bridge, homeless. Your Plan B may not be as desirable, may a different shift, different tasks, for a lower rate of pay. However, it should still be feasible, if not comfortable, and you are not living under a bridge.

Some people like to focus all their energy on Plan A and not even think a Plan B could be necessary. While that is a choice I could make, I suggest that having a good, solid Plan B makes life less uneasy when thoughts of losing that Plan A job flash across your mind. For example, my Plan A is to take a specific route to the next city. It is the road I want to take because it is the shortest and fastest. All well and good. Except there may be construction or an accident that makes that route unavailable at the time I want to travel. If I already prepared a good Plan B route, I could take a different way to get there. The road might not be as fast or as smooth; it may take a lot longer. But I can still end up where I wanted to be.

**Skill 7 Prevention and Planning**

To summarize skill 7 is about prevention and planning. Assessing the things that cause unease in your life and doing a risk assessment on them. - How likely is it, and how bad would it be. Then planning how to prevent the stressor and what is Plan B to survive and move forward if it did happen.

- Setting up your life to prevent common stressors.
- Looking ahead and planning how to manage risk.

*Peace.*

*It does not mean*

*to be in a place*

*where there is no*

*noise, trouble or hard work.*

*It means*

*to be in the midst*

*of those things*

*and still be calm*

*in your heart.*

*Unknown*

# CHAPTER ELEVEN

## A Calmer Life

### Putting it all together

You have read about seven important skills for being calmer. If you implement even a couple of those skills into your life, your life will become calmer. If you put half these skills to work for you, your life will be better, and if you implement all of them, you will have made your life dramatically calmer.

It takes motivation to get started learning new skills. A journey of a thousand miles begins with one step. A journey to a calmer life begins with one step. It can seem like there is an awful lot to learn and it may seem overwhelming to try to implement all these skills at once. The good news is that you can take your time and move toward a calmer life little by little. Learning and implementing even one skill will help you be calmer. What I suggest is to pick one skill that seems most doable to you and practice that one skill. Work on incorporating that skill into your life. When you are ready, start working on another skill. In this way, your life gets better and better as you learn and practice more calming skills, but you will not be overwhelmed trying to do too much at once. Give yourself time to grow into these skills in your life. Nobody learned how to tie their shoes the first time they did it. It is unlikely you just got on a bicycle and rode it well the first time. There are a lot of skills involved in this book. It does not really matter what order you learn them. Take your time and give yourself credit for every little improvement that you make, every time you make a choice that makes life calmer.

Here is a summary of the seven key skills to a calmer life.

**Skill 1 Managing** your body involves both your physical body state and your emotional body state since these feed on each other. When you intentionally manage your body, you are also influencing the state of your emotions. Building the skill of managing your body will give you more control over your state of calm or unease.

- Physical Calm - Practice good posture, walking, standing, or sitting.
- Emotional Body Calm - Breathe deeply.

**Skill 2 Managing Your Mind** – Mental Images, Selective Focus, Curiosity, and Laughter. Managing your mind, which involves intentionally creating and spending time with pleasant images, thoughts, focus and with laughter. When you intentionally manage your mind, you are also influencing the state of your emotions and your body.

- Spend time with pleasant mental images of nature.
- Selectively choose to focus on one thing
- Develop more curiosity about the world around you
- Laughter is good medicine

**Skill 3 Managing Your Thought Habits** which involves assessing your thinking patterns and deciding which habits are moving you toward unease and which ones are moving you toward calm. When you intentionally manage and change your thinking patterns you are also influencing your state of calm or unease.

- Assess your thinking patterns.
- Decrease negative thoughts.
- Increase positive and neutral thoughts.

**Skill 4 Technology and Your Focus**, which involves paying attention to the kind of media you allow into your mind. Be aware of the effect media tone has on your sense of unease or sense of calm. Then make changes to the way you interact with technology to move you toward being calmer.

- Be aware of how you are being entertained and informed.

- Look at where your passive attention is focused.
- Step away from technology periodically, give yourself a breather.
- Use technology to help you focus on a calmer life.

**Skill 5 Manage Your Attitude** is a vital skill of being calm. The way we approach life, our attitude greatly affects our feeling of calmness or uneasiness. The attitude of acceptance and gratefulness is important to contentment, which is the calm realization of how much you already have.

- Practice acceptance.
- Increase your gratefulness.
- Look for the beauty around you.

**Skill 6 Managing Core Values**. which includes learning to have integrity, the calmness of doing the right thing. Also, when life has stressful, difficult circumstances, learning to seek out the good that can come from challenging times. And practicing compassion for self and others.

- Increase the integrity in your life.
- Seek out and finding the good in the world.
- Practice compassion for yourself and for others.

**Skill 7 Prevention and Planning** Assessing the things that cause unease in your life and doing a risk assessment on them. - How likely is it, and how bad would it be. Then planning how to prevent the stressor and what is Plan B to survive and move forward if it did happen.

- Setting up your life to prevent common stressors.
- Looking ahead and planning how to manage risk.

Some of these skills may be easy to insert throughout your day, like taking a moment to sit up straight and breathe deeply. Some of the skills may seem too big to tackle at first. Those you can break down into smaller pieces to take step by step, or break down into small bits of time spent. Work on a step for ten focused minutes, then leave it alone till another time. Little by little, you can increase the calm in your life.

Planning is looking ahead at a goal and giving some thought of how to get there. James has decided he wants to walk to a tall mountain he sees in the distance. He is making that his long-term goal. He needs to be able to see the mountain now and then, so he knows he is headed in the right direction. There are also some big rivers between where he is and the mountain. So, he has to do some mid-range planning of how he will cross the rivers. But most of his time will be spent watching the path directly in front of him so he does not fall into potholes. In his planning, James thinks about the supplies he will need, the weather he may encounter, and the length of time the trip will take. He also gives some thought to unforeseen circumstances that could come up, what else he might need, and how to handle problems. With some good planning, James can calmly enjoy his journey, prepared for what may lie ahead.

Understand that it is normal to reach plateaus where after you have made a lot of progress, then progress slows or seems to stop. Just be patient with yourself to maintain what you have gained. Understand that when a plant grows, a lot of that growth is underground in the roots, and it takes time for it to show above ground. Plants need to put down strong roots before they can grow up and have more leaves and blooms. Give yourself time to grow strong roots. You have already made progress - because you have read through this book. You are already moving forward on your own journey to a calmer life.

By taking a positive and proactive approach toward learning the skills of keeping calm, you can open up opportunities to bring changes for the better for yourself and others; to improve confidence, and resilience. It may take some effort and time, but by making the decision to live calmly you can truly make changes that YOU want, that will take you to places you have always wanted to go, mentally, physically and spiritually.

In closing, I want to remind you that I have posted many free resources for you to continue your journey toward keeping calm on my website at FaithfulHabits.com/keepingcalm Please access these free resources.

*Like the flower that blooms*

*in the midst of snow*

*belief, trust and loyalty (faith)*

*endure through the*

*difficult seasons of life (winters)*

*Faith Winters*

# CHAPTER TWELVE

## Faith's Story of Keeping Calm

Decades of my life were spent living with uneasiness. I grew up in a Christian and abusive home. Christian and abusive should not be in the same sentence, but they were in my childhood. I grew up in the midst of extreme poverty, occasional homelessness, and all kinds of abuse. Calm is important to me because I grew up in a home without calm. I learned early that in the middle of being abused, having the outward appearance of calm made the abuse less severe. Those early lessons taught me the importance of outward calm even when the inward part was having a raging panic attack. But outward calm is not enough, and it is not what this book is about. This book has shown you the skills you can learn to have inward calm. I found that there is yet another source of calm for the inner core of my being: a relationship with the author of calm, the author of peace, Jesus.

There are four things I have always known even from my earliest memories. I have always known that God is. What could be known about God was plain to me as a child because God has made it plain to us. Since the creation of the world, God's invisible qualities—his eternal power and divine nature—have been clearly seen, being understood from what has been made. I could see His handiwork all around me. All the plants and trees and the intricacies of their beauty and diversity tell me of God. So, I have always known that God exists.

The second thing I have always known is that God loves me. I could see it in the nature around me, the way that He has created the world to give us delight. Food could just be for nourishment—and it does nourish—but food is also for delight. Our nourishment comes in such a wide variety of colors and flavors and smells and textures. I see that God loves us in the color of flowers. Whether purple or yellow or pink or white, there's such a huge array of color. What is the purpose of color but to bring delight to our hearts? We are created to respond to and take pleasure in beauty. Watching trees, the sight of all the different shapes leaves dancing in the wind, has always spoken to me of God's love for me. Later, I read the Bible which is filled with messages of His love.

The third thing I have always known is that I am safe in God's care. In the midst of the chaos around me as a little girl, dealing with abuse, poverty, and constantly moving, I knew I was safe in God's care. No matter what happened, He was there with me, is here with me, loves me, and cares for me. My present and my eternity are safe with Him.

The fourth thing I have always known is that although God exists, God loves me, and I am safe in His care, which does not keep me from having problems or getting hurt. I was hurt in body and heart a lot as a little girl. I was abused by the very people who should have protected me. Sometimes they behaved in ways that were loving and nurturing, but I could not rely on that. I knew that the betrayal of abuse was always a part of my experience with them. My family all worked as migrant farm laborers in fields and orchards. I started working full time at the age of three. We experienced discrimination and rejection from people around us. Also, I experienced ridicule and rejection from other kids in schools as the new kid, the poor kid who did not know what other kids knew and did not have what other kids had. I experienced the glaring disapproval of adults in grocery stores when we shopped, dirty, after a hard day's work to buy tonight's supper with today's wages.

In my understanding of how the world works is that God cherishes being loved and He gave us free will so that we could choose to love Him or choose not to love Him. That ability to choose is a precious thing. When we freely choose to love God, it is glorious. But God will not make us love Him; He invites us to love Him. He gave us free will, so we get to choose how we will live, what we will value. Therefore, some people use their free will to hurt themselves and hurt others. I was hurt a lot as a child by the choices of others. When I say that I am safe in God's care, I know that eternally I am safe. When I die, I will go to be with Him in heaven in that glorious presence. For everything my heart desires is there: my heart desires Him.

Where is God when I am wrongly hurt? God is nurturing me, giving me the strength to endure the hurt. He is holding my heart. Why did not He stop a little girl from being abused? He is all powerful; He could have prevented my pain. He chose not to stop it, but He gave me something better: the ability to endure, the resilience to live through it. Then, later in life, He gave me a healing process that healed all of those wounds, all of this pain from my childhood. And, more than that, He gave me a heart to want to help others who are in pain. A major part of my adult life is about helping others who are in pain.

Not only am I a theorist who has studied in Graduate School the theories of dysfunction and of healing and know the ways that we can be psychologically healed. I also have personally experienced suffering and healed through it. I have experienced that God designed us so we can heal. So, when I have a client in front of me who talks about the depth of their wounds and the trauma that they have endured, it resonates with me. I know what suffering feels like, but more importantly, I know what it feels like to heal and therefore I can hold hope for them. I can encourage them that I used to have PTSD (Post Traumatic Stress Disorder), but I do not have that anymore. I dealt with that for decades pretty intensely, but it has been gone now for decades too.

My experience shows me that when life is in chaos, God is here with me in the midst of that chaos, comforting my heart. Being safe in God's care does not mean He is going to protect me from the things going on in the world. It means He protects my heart and my mind; He gives me a way out, gives me a way to be resilient. I can still have the joy of being loved by God no matter what is happening. Happiness is a feeling of contentment and satisfaction or of intense pleasure. Joy, though, is not based on what is happening in the moment or if things are going well or not. Joy is a stronger feeling acquired by something great or wonderful, something happening now or something we anticipate in the future. We can have joy even in the midst of suffering. I have joy knowing that God loves me, knowing that I will be with Him in eternity in heaven. I have had joy in the very midst of all the sadness, chaos, and turmoil of my life because I know who holds my heart.

## THE EXPLOSION HAPPENED AT 9:38 AM.

### The story of a kidney transplant day.

*Mother of the kidney transplant recipient version.*

*7:30 am* That morning I (Faith) was in a pre-planning meeting at the City Hall offices to begin the permit process for an extensive remodel on my house. My son and his wife and I were going to share a home together, so I was adding a second floor to my house so there would be plenty of space for us. I was in this meeting with city officials going over the plans of what I wanted to do. It was a huge project, and I was excited and a little nervous about it. In this meeting were four city officials and me. The whole situation provoked some anxiety within me. While I was trying to listen to what they were telling me I needed to do, my phone went off.

*8:20 am* The officials all looked at me as I pulled out my loudly ringing phone. I glanced at who it was as I silenced it and I set the phone face down on the table in front of me. It was my son. My phone is always on, because I supervise graduate student intern counselors and if they have a client emergency where they need to contact me, I'm on call for them. Also, over the past ten years my phone is always on in case my son has a medical emergency and needs to contact me. Because he has had some medical issues and been in the hospital a number of times over the years. It has been a few years since he has called me for an emergency, since he is married now he calls his wife, not me. So it has been two or three years since he has called me for a medical emergency. We had this protocol for his emergency calls. As a counselor and clinical supervisor, I spend most of my work life in confidential meetings. So I often am not available to answer a phone call.

Timothy and I had agreed years ago that when he had an emergency what he would call me, leave a message on what he needs and then he would hang up. Then he'll call me back again and hang up. Because when I'm in meetings as a counselor I'm not going to interrupt the meeting by answering the phone. When he calls me the second time I'm going to tell the people I'm with about our code that he will call me three times. And I'll need to answer the phone because it will be an emergency.

Well, we are 10 minutes from the end of this meeting with the city officials and he's called me once and then it was long enough he probably left me a voicemail. Then he has called me twice and he hung up, quickly enough that there is probably no voicemail. So I'm telling the people in the meeting about my code with my son. But he doesn't call a third time. I'm still a little nervous because I'm in this meeting trying to figure out the next steps on my big project. When he doesn't call the third time I continue in the meeting since there were only ten minutes left till the end. Then I go out to my car.

*8:35 am.* I listen to the message Timothy left on my voicemail. "Mom, I got the call!" That's all he says, and I'm like, "What call?" My mind is still filled with the details of the meeting I just left. I'm trying to figure this out and what does his message mean.

When he calls me back, he repeats himself. "Mom, I got the call!"

"What call?"

He replies, "For the kidney transplant."

All of a sudden my adrenaline flashes up and I am on high alert.

A deceased donor kidney has become available. We have been waiting for three years for this call. The kidney transplant team required that Timothy have a number of people to call for transportation if he gets a call for an available kidney. The viability time for a deceased donor kidney is a short window. I am one of the people he has for back-up transportation. "What do you need from me?" I ask. He tells me that his wife's aunt is on her way over to drive him to the hospital and his wife will join him there in a few hours. He wants me to meet him there. I say I will come right away. I hang up and I start crying.

Over three years beforehand, Timothy's kidneys had started to fail. It became clear with his end-stage kidney failure that he would be on thrice-weekly dialysis the rest of his life unless he got a kidney transplant. Dialysis treatments take 3 or 4 hours per session to do some things done by healthy kidneys: removing waste products and excess fluid from the blood. Without working kidneys, toxins would build up in his blood, making his skin a grayish hue and his mind seemed sluggish. On the day of dialysis it would get better, but the toxins would build up again.

Getting the call for a donor kidney after three years led to intense feelings and a swirled mixture of relief that finally he will get a kidney to have a more normal life again. Gratitude that a donor kidney was available. The excitement that his life would be open to such possibilities. Stress because there were so many things involved in this. My adrenaline spiked, making me highly activated and emotional. So I sat up straight and started breathing deeply (Calming Skill 1), lowering my stress a little so I could plan what I needed to do. I contacted a friend of ours to tell her that Timothy's transplant was happening and ask her to please call our church and our other friends to ask them to pray. I contacted my work to let them know I would not be coming in. Since my son had his ride and he will get to the hospital in about 45 minutes or so, and I was only about 20 minutes away, I took a few extra minutes to calm down before I started driving.

The hospital is downtown and there were a few different routes I could use to get there. I planned (Calming Skill 7) the best route to take. Usually I take the freeway straight into the city. But knowing I was distracted and so highly activated, I decided to stay off of the freeway to avoid driving fast. I planned to go a slower, therefore safer, route through more residential neighborhoods. I had my plan. I asked my friends for support. Then it was time to drive. My mind went all kinds of places, though, distracting me. I found myself almost by default on the freeway onramp with no way to get off.

Okay, change of plans. I was going to have to take the freeway, but that was all right. I could take the freeway to the first exit and proceed from there. I drove 45 miles an hour in the right-hand lane. I tried to keep myself calm, remembering to breathe, focusing on driving safely, watching traffic, and spacing. Then I missed the exit. All it took was a few seconds of being distracted by intense thoughts. So I had to go all the way to the city on the freeway. The next exit would put me into the heart of the busiest part of the city, but I could drive across to the hospital from there easy enough, I was familiar with the route. At the base of the off ramp, I saw this guy with a hand-lettered sign saying, "Homeless please help." Thinking about the needs of others helps me to calm down (Calming Skill 6). So I gave this guy $20 as I made that turn into the heart of the city.

*8:58 am* Driving on city streets feels stressful to me. They feel too narrow and too crowded. People step out in front of you all the time. Under normal circumstances, I have to be intentional when I'm driving in the city due to the driving stress I feel. This day was not normal. I drove across midtown, trying to go west toward the hospital, when suddenly there was an emergency vehicle right behind me!

Lights flashed and sirens blared. My heart lurched and I found a place to pull over and get out of the way. Sudden sirens have a tendency to activate a little bit of adrenaline in me and I already had my adrenaline activated, so that was extra stressful. When that emergency vehicle had gone past me, I breathed deeply and pulled back out onto the road. After five more blocks, I stopped at the light to turn left and suddenly there was a big fire truck, with full lights and sirens crossing right in front of me. Eventually I made my turn toward the hospital, then I heard another emergency vehicle heading west, but at least it wasn't on my street. A few minutes later, another fire truck. All of these were going generally in the direction I was headed. I thought, "I hope they are not going to the hospital where Timothy is." I concentrated on getting there safely to join my son. The parking garage was a block away from the hospital, on the far side of a medical office building. I found one of the few remaining spaces, which happened to be on the same level as the walkway into the medical building.

*9:35 am* This medical building was actually where his kidney transplant doctor's office is. Timothy had brought me there to meet his transplant doctors as one of his required support team. I stopped in there and they told me where to go in the hospital to find Timothy. I walked through those hallways and down the noisy elevator when I heard a big thump in the distance through the elevator and walls, but I barely noticed because I was focused on getting to my son. The long walk was good exercise to calm me down.

In the hospital waiting room sat my daughter-in-law's aunt. She told me how Timothy was doing and where he was in a room waiting for the doctors. I had to lean close to hear her because in the far end of the waiting room the TV blared loudly with breaking news about some emergency, with fire trucks behind the reporter. I ignored the TV as I left the waiting room because, the news is always about trouble, and I did not have the extra energy to pay attention to media inputs right then. I chose to selectively focus only on what was most important to me: my son and what he needs (Calming Skill 4). His wife was not there yet. I sat with Timothy, seeing how he was doing and being there to support him.

Then a nurse came in to talk to him, asking if he was excited to be finally getting this kidney transplant. She asked him about his history with surgeries. He gave her the details about each of those. I sat there quietly, calm and supportive. It brought up for me every traumatic time we have ever dealt with in hospitals. The nurse went away, and we were both left with those memories fresh in our minds. Sitting next to my son in a hospital awaiting surgery is a familiar place for me. He was born 8 weeks early and I sat by him in the neonatal intensive care unit for 9 weeks. Over the next five years, there were three more surgeries. In his late teens, there were another two surgeries. So at that moment we were both seeing the sights, hearing the sounds, and smelling the smells similar to all those other times of stress. Even with the good outcomes we had, they are uneasy memories.

*10:14 am* Another nurse came to check his vitals and to ask again about his previous surgeries. She was wrapping up when suddenly the hospital fire alarm went off. Lights flashing, alarms sounding! We are both startled, looking to the nurse for what to do next. She calmly looked at us and at the alarm and said, "I think it's okay, I think it is just the smoke from down the street got in here. You stay here I will go check and be right back."

We waited on high alert. I thought about how a kidney transplant has this small window of time that a donated organ is viable. If this were a fire, and we had to evacuate, it was unlikely there would be time to find another operating room to make this transplant work. If that happened, he may have to wait years longer for another chance.

He must have been thinking similar thoughts because he said,

"It's the worst possible time for the fire alarm to go off."

I replied, "No, the worst time would have been if you were cut open on the operating table."

But it was still a bad time because this was where the doctors are, and where the operating room and surgery were scheduled. Thinking he may lose this opportunity was distressing.

Also, was there a fire? Were we safe in this building? The fire alarm was still blaring. After a few of the longest minutes of our lives, the nurse popped back in for a minute to tell us it was all right; there was no fire in the hospital, just smoke from a fire down the street. We could breathe again. The transplant could still take place today.

Finally the hospital fire alarm stopped flashing and the alarm shut off, and we were again left in a welcome silence to wait.

***The explosion had happened at 9:38 am.***

*A massive explosion, apparently ignited by a natural gas leak, ripped through a building in a popular downtown shopping district, causing destruction and injuring eight people, including three firefighters. Thankfully, no one was killed.*

*A natural gas leak was reported at 8:55 am in a downtown business area where some construction was in progress. Minutes later, emergency vehicles with more than 100 firefighters plus crews from the gas utility company converged on the site, evacuating all the buildings in the area.*

*The explosion happened at 9:38 am, the utility reported. The building that contained a bagel shop, a tattoo parlor, and an eyewear business was totally destroyed, while a spa and condo building next door sustained heavy damage.*

*The hospital was six blocks away and was not damaged by the blasts or the resulting fires. Smoke was drifting thickly over that part of the city.*

*I was seven blocks away and going down in a noisy elevator at the time of the blast. That was the muffled thump, and extra vibration which my brain accepted as normal for this older elevator, and I had given it no thought, being focused on finding my son.*

I actively worked to stay calm, using all the calming skills I knew so I could be supportive of my son. Yet another medical professional came in, an anesthesiologist or somebody. She greeted us and asked me if I was happy he was getting his transplant today. I nodded slightly. She went on to ask Timothy those same questions about all of the other traumatic things he had experienced in this type of environment. She was smiling and bubbly while I thought to myself, happy? 'Happy' was not the word, because I knew that for my son to get this transplant meant somebody else has died. Some other family had just experienced a sudden tragedy and they were heartbroken, grieving their loss. Their life turned upside down because they lost a loved one, and you want to know if I am happy? I could not be happy with that anonymous family in such grief. Donor kidneys are not a product off a shelf. They are the result of someone's sorrow. I was not feeling happy; grateful is the word. I was so very grateful. Grateful someone chose to be a donor; grateful my son was getting a kidney. But I was not happy. I didn't say this to her, and I didn't cry because my goal was to be a calm support for my son and his wife. But I prayed for my son and for that family and these were the thoughts swirling inside of me.

Timothy had asked to have the chaplain come by and pray with us. As Christians, God is an important part of our lives. When the young hospital chaplain arrived, he asked Timothy if he was religious and if he would like him to pray. Timothy answered yes and the three of us bowed our heads as the chaplain began to pray. As he spoke I had no idea who this guy was talking to. Maybe he was spiritual, but I did not feel any spirit of Christianity in him. He was being so politically correct that for all I knew he was talking to the ceiling. I felt no comfort from this guy being there and when he left I felt a sense of relief.

Rachael, his wife, got there soon after, so we both sat with Timothy at this point. I appreciate this woman so much. She sees who my son is with his strengths and faults and has been faithfully with him through many happy times and several struggling times. She is exactly the kind of Christian woman I prayed my son would marry, starting from when he was six years old. She is kind and generous, the natural result of a loving, healthy extended family network. Her mother and two more of her aunts are now in the waiting room as well.

Two o'clock came and went and the transplant doctor still hadn't shown up. An older gentleman came in, a pastor Timothy's wife knows. He was a stranger to me. He asked if he could pray with us. My daughter-in-law said, "Yes, please." We all bowed, and he started praying. I didn't know him, but instantly I knew his spirit and that he was a brother Christian. When he prayed with us, I knew he was praying to the God I love, the God who supports and cares for us, and the God who was walking with us through the midst of this troubling time. By the time we got to "Amen," my heart was calmer, and I felt the joy of His presence.

*3:15 pm* Eventually the transplant doctor came and talked with Timothy and again asked all those questions about the traumatizing times we've had in the hospitals before. Again, I'm asked if I'm happy about the transplant and I just nodded silently. The doctor told us they would come to take Timothy to surgery soon, then he left.

The Christian brother was still there with us, encouraging us when they came to take Timothy away for the surgery. I felt so comforted when that godly man began to sing: "God bless you, go with

God, through all eternity, my prayer will always be, may you go with God, till we meet again."

*3:30 pm* I had left the house at 6:30 am this morning. I've been at Timothy's side since 9:45 am. It would be many hours before Timothy is out of surgery. Neither Rachael nor I had much in the way of breakfast this morning and noon had come and gone. We found her family, and the six of us went to find a late lunch in the hospital cafeteria.

Of course, the cafeteria is closed. It was the middle of the afternoon and at the hospital maybe people don't eat in the middle of the afternoon. Rachael and I sat in the empty dining room, emotionally drained, tired, and hungry. Her mother and aunts left to see what might be available. They came back empty-handed; everything is closed. However, they sat down and started to pull resources out of their bags. One had some cheese sticks and apple slices, another some cans of soda, another some nuts. We were sustained by their nourishing love and care, and some strengthening snacks.

These women are part of an extended family of about thirty people, the grown children, spouses, and grandchildren of a loving, generous Christian couple who raised six children. Rachael is one of the fourteen grandchildren. When Rachael and Timothy got married, they not only welcomed him into the family; they welcomed me as well. Every person in that family knows they are loved and accepted. I have been blessed to join their monthly family gatherings.

These women brought food, so we had something to eat if we needed it. They sat with us as the surgery went on for hours. When the cafeteria finally reopened they made sure we had dinner and eventually we went upstairs to visit the chapel because we wanted a quiet place to pray. We went to the waiting room for the recovery area, and Rachael's dad and siblings joined us there. We all waited for the news of Timothy and prayed for him and supported each other. A phone call came for Rachael, and she's told the surgery is about half done and it's going well; everything's going fine.

*7:00 pm* The surgeon came by to tell is all was well, a routine operation, and it will be another hour or so before Timothy was brought to the recovery section.

*9:00 pm* Timothy was brought out of surgery to the Critical Care Unit. A nurse comes into the waiting room where we all were sitting together. Knowing that someone would be able to go in and see him in just a few minutes after they get him settled in the recovery room had the room full of excitement. My son had had surgery yet again, and now that he was out of surgery someone can go in and see him. But this time it would not be me. I had been with him through all of those other surgeries and after each surgery I'd been there to see him as soon as he came out of surgery. But this time, it wasn't me, because he is married so his wife would go in, as it should be. My heart as a mother grieved that for a moment, but I was content. He was with the one who loves him most. I accepted years ago that when he came to love this woman, I ceased to be the most important woman in his life. As it should be. About 30 minutes later, this kind and loving woman came out to get me and bring me in to see my son. I could clearly see that he was not only doing okay, but also better than he had been in a few years. His skin color was better, less grey and more toward pink already as his new kidney worked to clear the toxins out of his body. And even though he was still a little groggy from the surgery, I could see that already his mind was clearer, and he was more alert. My heart rested. Rachael would stay with him overnight and I would come to sit with him tomorrow. It was time for me to go home.

*11:30 pm* I got home, emotionally exhausted. This day was finally over. My son had a new kidney and was getting better. Over the next few days, he returned to health quickly as his new kidney cleaned up his body and got rid of excess waste.

As I think back to that day, I can see that I used most of the calming skills I have taught you about in this book, and a few others. Using the calming skills allowed me to survive an extremely taxing day and remain a calming presence for my son and daughter-in-law.

A lot of my own life has been uncertain and hard. But I have seen God's love and care in the midst of hard places. When I would call out to Him, He would comfort my heart, comfort my mind. I read His word and in there the words of comfort for other people who have struggled. When I am connected to God's people in church groups and home Bible study groups, these people would care about me. We are made to be connected to others in the body of Christ. It is kind of God's love with flesh on.

God loves me even when life is not what I like. God seems to be more concerned with my character development than with my comfort. I tend to be more concerned with my comfort. I like to be comfortable, but it is in the uncomfortable times that my character can develop. In those times, I get to choose if am I going to stay true to God and my integrity, if am I going to do what is right and proper even when things are hard. I get to choose if am I going to love and trust God when life is hard.

Jesus is the way. John 3:16 states that God so loved the world that He sent His only son that whosoever believes in Him should not perish but have eternal life. I find that such a wonderfully comforting statement. The "whosoever" means this offer is open to anybody and everybody. The offer is something we have to accept in order to have that eternal life He offers. No one is too bad or too wrong or too different. God made all of us. When we accept Jesus as Savior and Lord, we are agreeing with God that we have done wrong. Confessing to Him what it is that we have done, and then accepting Him into our life as Lord and Savior, gives us salvation. The Lord part means that then I want to obey Him. He is not going to make me obey Him, but because I love Him because He loves me, I want to obey. So, I spend time reading His word. I spend time with His people, so I am connected and growing more like Him.

This invitation to abundant life is open to anyone and everyone. Not everyone chooses to accept Jesus as Lord and Savior, but that is who He is in my life. He is the author of peace. That core source of calm is what God gives us in the midst of life's troubles. He is the author of calm, the source of calm.

All of the skills I taught you in this book will help you tremendously to have more calm. They will help you to be able to walk with calm inside and outside as you go through the trials of life. But the deepest calm, that solid unshakable calm welling inside of you, is that which comes from knowing, loving, and following Jesus.

**Are you ready to make lasting change?**

**Get the new KEEPING CALM workbook to help strengthen your specific calm goals.**

This companion workbook shows you step by step how to develop and strengthen the key skills for living a calmer life using easy-to-follow exercises

**KEEPING CALM is also available:**

- on Kindle
- Audiobook
- Hardcover

www.faithfulhabits.com/keepingcalm

Check out our website for other books by this author and other Free resources

## Companion Books

## The Trauma Healing Series

**Trauma Healing Series - Book 1**

**FUNDAMENTALS**

*Escape the Lingering Effects*
*of Bullying, Abuse or Trauma*

By learning your fundamental human rights, developing inner awareness of your strengths, and understanding the contrast to past chaos you will step into a life with security, significance, and happiness. Explore how to have more peace within yourself, better relationships with others, and more freedom and contentment, no matter what is going on around you.

FaithfulHabits.com/books

**Trauma Healing Series - Book 2**

**RESTORATION**

*Living as Designed, in Joy and Peace*

You are designed to have peace and joy and be able to heal from the wounds of life. Look deeply into your uniqueness. Put to rest the old wounds that hinder your healing and trap you into painful patterns of responding to life. By exploring and adopting healthy patterns instead, you will live your best life after trauma. You will have restoration.

FaithfulHabits.com/books

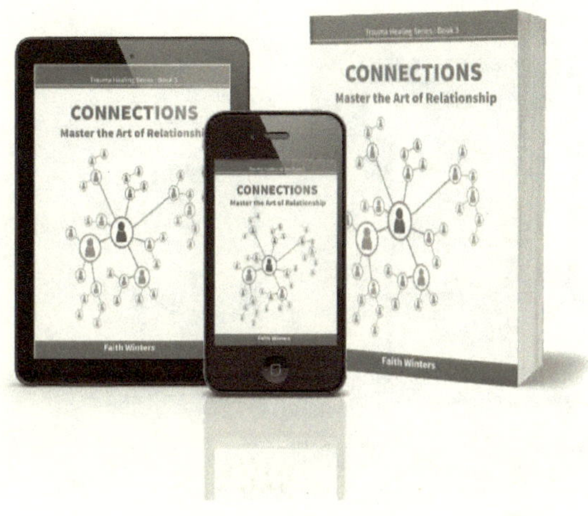


**Trauma Healing Series - Book 3**

**CONNECTIONS**

*Master the Art of Relationship*

When you do what it takes to develop wholesome social habits and essential boundary skills, you can have good relationships at home, at work, and with friends, family, and that special someone, no matter what your past relationships were like. By learning key skills for a healthy lifestyle and safe, healthy relationships, you will unlock the power of community to discover your connected place in the world.

FaithfulHabits.com/books

**Trauma Healing Series - Book 4**

**ABUNDANCE**

*Create Confidence, Contentment and Happiness*

You can have the freedom of contentment, recognizing and enjoying the abundance of life around you. Contentment is not the fulfillment of what you want but the realization of what you already have. By using the principles of abundance in this book, you will derive riches that go far beyond the temporary rewards of success and create lasting happiness in any situation.

FaithfulHabits.com/books

Other books by Faith Winters

Coming in 2021

**Motivated!**

**The Helper's Journey Series**

**Book 1 - Compassionate Presence**

**Book 2 – Compassionate Leadership**

**Book 3 - Compassion Fatigue**

**Book 4 – The Trouble with Compassion**

Coming soon:

Workbooks for each of the trauma Healing Series

Online classes for each of the chapters of the Trauma Healing Series.

To ask how your group or organization can apply for discounts and scholarships contact us at info@faithfulhabits.com

www.ingramcontent.com/pod-product-compliance
Lightning Source LLC
LaVergne TN
LVHW090952080826
845145LV00003B/976

* 9 7 8 1 7 3 6 7 3 6 7 0 8 *